Theirs not to do or die . . .

Tony Brehony

KB
KESTREL BOOKS
Book Publishers & Distributors

Also by the author

West Cork, 'a sort of a history, like . . .'

Journalist, short-story writer and broadcaster, Tony Brehony looks back down through the swirling mist of history, fable, myth and tale which all make up the glorious heritage of his native West Cork.

Dedicated

to

a much-maligned group of gentlemen

THE ROYAL NAVY'S CHIEF PUSSERS

in

World War Two

First published 1999
by

KESTREL BOOKS

48A Main St., Bray, Co. Wicklow, Ireland.
Tel: +353 1 2863402; Fax: +353 1 2860984
Email: sales@kestrelbooks.com

Printed in Ireland by
Falcon Print & Finish Ltd.

ISBN:
Pbk: 1-900505-46-0

Copyright for text © Tony Brehony
Copyright for typesetting, layout, © Kestrel Books Ltd.

This novel is entirely a work of fiction. The names, characters and incidents portrayed in it are the work of the author's imagination. Any resemblance to actual persons, living or dead, events or localities is entirely coincidental.

All rights reserved. No part of this book may be reproduced or utilised in any form or by any means electronic or mechanical, including photography, filming, recording, video recording, photocopying or by any information storage and retrieval system, or shall not by way of trade or otherwise, be lent, resold or otherwise circulated in any form of binding of cover other than that in which it is published, without prior permission in writing from the publisher. The moral rights of the author have been asserted.

"Don't talk to me about naval tradition. It's nothing but rum, sodomy and the lash."

Winston Spencer Churchill

Contents

The Beginning 1
The Bristol Channel 15
Portsmouth 31
Liverpool 43
The Irish Sea 57
The Northern Approaches 63
The Atlantic 73
Bermuda 85
Malta 97
Norfolk Va 111
New York 123
Gibraltar and Sicily 133
Normandy 145
Germany 157
The End 175
Epilogue 179

CHAPTER ONE

THE BEGINNING

Commander Louis Taylor, Royal Naval Volunteer Reserve, Captain of His Majesty's Ship Manway, strode down the cobbled jetty, his mouth grim, hands behind his back, left wrist locked in his right fist. Man and boy he had sailed the oceans of the world and, in his prime, commanded some of the finest vessels of the Cunard line. And all that for what? - to be called out of retirement to listen to horseshit from a jumped-up admiral of the Royal Navy? His so-called superior, no less! Good Christ Almighty, the man's nothing but a stupid wanker - if he's even capable of that! Wouldn't last a month in the Merchant Navy! A fucking week more likely!

 Commander Taylor realised that he was mouthing the words aloud and looked around to make sure there was nobody within earshot. To entertain thoughts that his Commander-in-Chief was a stupid wanker was tantamount to mutiny. To actually say it aloud, Jesus, they'd count that as treason...

 HMS Manway was a sleek 900-ton luxury yacht built for the pleasures of peacetime. Her slim lines peaked to a brazen female figurehead with flowing hair cascading around her shoulders to merge with the rusting grey hull. Full wooden tits jutted temptingly in lecherous invitation to every sailor who joined her. Captain Taylor's eyes lifted and for a moment he stared, eyeball to eyeball, into the smirking face. The tip of her tongue showed through wide panting lips parted in what he was quite satisfied was a shuddering frenzy of orgasmic climax. Shaking his head sadly, he grimaced in disgust and strode towards the after brow.

Now fitted for war in October 1940, HMS Manway sported a four-inch gun on her quarterdeck and a brace of Oerlikon twenty-millimetre cannon on her bridge. Despite this display of armament, and whatever his C-in-C might think, Captain Taylor knew that the ship he commanded looked more like a sea-going tart than a man-of-war anxious and ready to do or die for King and Country.

Manway's crew, unlike the captain, was extremely proud of the blowsy figurehead. They had christened her Wally on the doubtful authority of a dockyard welder who claimed that the yacht was once owned by the Prince of Wales in those heady pre-war days when His Royal Highness chased Wallis Simpson up and down the Med, and around the Greek islands.

The boson's pipe shrilled and Lieutenant Ferguson, Royal Naval Volunteer Reserve, waited at the after brow to greet his captain. Earlier that morning Captain Taylor had confided in his First Lieutenant that he was going to ask the C-in-C's permission to have the figurehead removed.

'I can't take it any more, Number One,' he'd confessed. 'I feel like a bloody pimp every time I bring this ship in and out of harbour. It's that painted whore up there flashing her tits on the bow. I know damn well that other ships are whistling her up rather than saluting a fellow-fighting man-of-war. They're laughing at us, I tell you, and it's not good for morale. She'll have to go.'

Ferguson came to attention and saluted. Taylor's return salute was perfunctory. 'Successful meeting I trust, sir?' Ferguson ventured hopefully.

Captain Taylor's licked his dry lips. He took Ferguson's arm and led him across the quarterdeck out of earshot of the boson's mate. His hands gripped the wire rail, his knuckles white.

'You won't believe what that - that...' He managed to recover his composure before becoming guilty of engaging a junior officer in a mutinous conversation. He squared his shoulders. 'Permission refused, I'm afraid, Number One,' he told Ferguson. 'C-in-C refused point blank to have that ...that - the figurehead removed.' He sighed. 'He said that Admiral Nelson had a figurehead on the Victory, and Sir Francis Drake and Sir Walter Raleigh and Christ knows who else all had figureheads on their vessels, and he thought that we reserve chappies should be proud to be in such illustrious company, and...' His voice choked. 'And d'you know something else, Number One? It cost me three large gins to have to listen to a half an hour of that fucking shit.'

Captain Taylor pulled has cap tightly down over his close-cropped greying hair and stormed up the ladder towards his sea-cabin. The soft strains of

Moonlight Sonata drifted from the scuttle of what in peacetime had been the after stateroom, now used as the crew's recreation quarters. Taylor stopped, his cup of misery overflowing. That damned piano was another thing he'd tried to have removed when Manway was preparing for war. A fucking piano on a man-of-war! Jesus Christ!

The dockyard authorities, however, overruled him. The instrument, they pointed out, was a full-sized Steinway concert piano that couldn't be moved without major alterations to the vessel's superstructure. Whether or not Captain Taylor wanted a Steinway on board his ship, like the figurehead, he was stuck with it. As far as he could understand, it seemed that the ship had been built around the fucking thing.

He looked back down at Ferguson. 'Who's that?' he asked. 'I thought there was nobody aboard who could play that thing,' He listened for a minute in silence. 'Tone deaf meself, I'm afraid. Able to play, is he?'

Ferguson nodded enthusiastically. 'Oh, yes sir! Quite good actually. He's our new Supply Assistant. Joined us yesterday to take over victualling duties from the Coxswain. O'Neill's his name. Irish.'

The captain nodded. 'I see. Good. I hope he knows something about victualling a ship's company. Playing that fucking piano won't keep them fed.' He headed for his sea-cabin. 'Oh, by the way, Number One,' he said, pausing and jerking his thumb towards the figurehead. He removed his cap and rubbed around the inside band thoughtfully. 'That - that thing up there on the prow, I know I can leave it in your capable hands to -er- look after it. After all, the way the C-in-C feels about it, we wouldn't want it to get lost overboard some dark stormy night, now would we? If you see what I mean...' His voice trailed off and the cabin door closed behind him.

Ferguson's lips pursed thoughtfully. A shrewd officer, now nearing his 29th birthday, and hoping to get his own command soon, he knew it would enhance his chances if he could help his captain in any way. In fact, it's my duty, he thought. And yes sir, I do see what you mean. Yes, indeed! And Coxswain Hardy was the obvious man to handle such a delicate task with just the right degree of discretion. He'd have a quiet word with him about it. If I ever manage to catch him sober, that is....

Unaware of the fact that his captain was listening to his recital, Supply Assistant James O'Neill sat happily at the Steinway lost in the joys of Beethoven. His fingers danced over the keys, brown eyes closed in rapturous delight. His fair head bowed and swayed to the rhythm of his music. He had never before played on such a magnificent instrument and he was both shocked and delighted when Lieutenant Ferguson handed him the key and appointed him official guardian of the Steinway. From that moment on O'Neill regarded the piano as his own.

The ship's tannoy rattled and a boatswain's call drowned out the soulful recital. 'D'ye hear there? Duty part of the watch and Supply Assistant O'Neill muster at the for'ard brow. At the double!'

O'Neill jumped in surprise. Just four months in His Majesty's Royal Navy, most of which had been spent in Portsmouth barracks aimlessly marching hither and thither, forming fours and fixing bayonets, it was the first time he had ever been called over the ship's tannoy and he wasn't sure where the for'ard brow was, or even what it was. He sighed and gently closed the piano lid, lovingly rubbing off a speck of dust with his sleeve. What, he wondered in anxious dismay, could possible require his presence at this for'ard brow? And at the double!

The duty watch was already assembled on the jetty under the supervision of Leading Seaman Tom Stevens, recently recalled from his civilian job as assistant commissioner at the Odeon cinema. Stevens didn't like being wakened up from his grog-induced afternoon nap but he cheered up considerably when he saw that the stores truck alongside had twenty stone jars as part of its mixed cargo. The red rings painted around the collars clearly indicated that they contained rum.

If he played his cards right with the new Jack Dusty - the naval nickname for supply assistants - there might be a sipper or two of bubbly to lull him back to slumberland where the Manway and this bloody war could soon be forgotten.

'Chop, chop then Dusty lad,' he called when the reluctant supply assistant appeared uncertainly at the brow. 'Let's get this fuckin' lot checked in so's we can all get back to the wank-sacks for some shut-eye.'

O'Neill felt the unwelcome colour flush to his cheeks. Born in Co. Meath and educated from the age of four to eighteen by a succession of nuns and priests, any reference to sex caused him acute embarrassment.

Sex, it had been drummed into him by Sister Angela of the Convent of the Immaculate Conception, was a grave sin whether in thought, word or - she could hardly bring herself to say it - in deed. After four months of navy life O'Neill still wasn't used to the fact that every second word spoken by His Majesty's sailors seemed to have something to do with sex.

Just then Coxswain Bert Hardy, his eyes also heavy with sleep, arrived at the brow. Like Stevens, on the outbreak of war he had been recalled from his civilian job as postman in Bournemouth to defend his king and country from the onslaught of Hitler's hordes, a task which Captain Taylor considered was singularly unfitted for an alcoholic

Apart from being responsible for the maintenance of good order and discipline at all times, the coxswain took the wheel at action stations when entering and leaving harbour. On some of the smaller ships in the fleet he also undertook the victualling of the crew and the distribution of the rum rations. However, when Captain Taylor realised that his coxswain seemed to have access to an endless supply of alcohol, whether on land or on sea, he immediately arranged for a supply assistant to be drafted to the ship.

Hardy took the supply notes from O'Neill, his rheumy gaze quickly running down the list. He nodded in satisfaction when he saw twenty jars of rum listed.

'Ah good. These are the supplies I ordered last week,' he told O'Neill. 'That'll be your job from now on.' He looked out at the duty part of the watch who had started to unload the lorry. 'Where's tanky?'

O'Neill's eyebrows lifted. 'T-tanky?'

Coxswain Hardy blew his nose noisily. 'Jesus,' he said loudly enough for everybody to hear, 'I don't know what this fucking navy's coming to. Don't you Jack Dustys know anything? Tanky Blake - the able seaman detailed to help you in the stores. He's called tanky - all tankies are called tanky for Christ sake.' He raised his eyes to heaven and turned to the grinning quartermaster. 'Pipe Able Seaman Blake to the for'ard brow at the double. And send someone down to the wardroom for the officer of the watch - we'll need the keys of the spirit room.'

Hardy took O'Neill's arm in a friendly grasp. 'You're a nice boy, Jack lad,' he said conspiratorially, 'and I know and you know that you know sweet fuck-all about this job, but you can rely on me to see you right. Okay? Just you do exactly as I tell you and you'll soon get the hang of it. But watch it!' He pointed at the overalled seamen unloading the lorry on the jetty. 'Those bastards out there'll pinch the eyes out of your head, given half a chance. And the same goes for that dockyard shower. Check every item on that list and make sure it's delivered before you sign for it. Okay?'

O'Neill winced when the coxswain's grip tightened on his arm. The voice had dropped to a whisper. 'But the hardest part of the job, Jack lad, is to see that the stuff gets from here down to the storeroom. You'd want eyes in your arse to watch a British sailor when he's humping stores through the mess-decks.'

Tanky Blake, the three stripes on his left arm indicating that he had already served over 14 years in the navy without getting caught doing something he shouldn't have done, arrived breathless at the brow.

The coxswain scowled at him. 'Where the hell do you think you are, eh? On your daddy's fucking yacht? Didn't you hear the duty watch being called out to take on stores?'

Tanky grinned apologetically and said nothing. After nine months working with the coxswain he knew that it was impossible to reason with him until a few shots of rum in his system got his alcoholic content up to something near normal.

Lieutenant Ferguson arrived with the keys of the spirit room. Coxswain Hardy came to attention and saluted, his heels coming together with a loud click. Ferguson returned the salute, his heart sinking. When Hardy acted in what the navy called 'pusser' fashion, there was usually something untoward afoot. Now he'd have to keep a weather eye open for all sorts of trouble and he'd been looking forward so much to an undisturbed afternoon watch. He purposely addressed his orders to O'Neill to make it quite clear to him that checking the stores and getting them safely aboard was now solely the supply assistant's responsibility and not the coxswain's.

'Check the rum off the lorry first, O'Neill, and get it aboard. I'll carry on below and get the spirit room opened.'

'Aye, aye, sir,' said Coxswain Hardy and saluted again. Ferguson sighed audibly and carried on aft. Hardy turned to Leading Seaman Stevens and shouted to him to start getting the jars of rum on board at the double.

'You take charge here on the jetty, O'Neill,' he ordered, 'and make bloody sure that everything that comes off that lorry comes over the brow and down to the store. Tanky, you carry on down to the store and see to it that everything is checked in and stored shipshape and Bristol fashion.' He clapped his hands together to generate some action. 'Carry on then! Chop, chop!'

Wiping his sleeve across his mouth, he looked after the lieutenant now disappearing down the after hatch. 'I'd better go down below to the spirit room with the Jimmy,' he told the quartermaster. 'He'll never find it on his own.'

Ferguson was looking around the spirit room when Coxswain Hardy came bustling in. There were three full casks of rum lashed to rings attached to the bulkhead and seven gallon jars stacked like wine bottles on sloping racks. Twelve empty jars and two empty casks had been put to one side awaiting return to the dockyard.

'I'll get these empties out of the way, sir,' Hardy offered, 'so we'll have a bit of room in here to manoeuvre.' He rolled the two empty casks onto the open space outside the spirit room.

Lieutenant Ferguson had been considering the Captain's suggestion about getting rid of the figurehead. Now that he was alone with the coxswain, it seemed as good a time as any to raise the delicate subject of its disposal once and for all.

'I say, Coxswain,' he started, keeping his back to Hardy and pretending to examine the capacity markings on a cask, 'you know that damned figurehead? The Captain was wondering if there's anything you...aah...we could do about it...er...sort of detaching it and, well, losing the damned thing overboard...'

Hardy had quietly lifted a full jar of rum from the rack with one hand while he noisily rattled two empties along the deck with the other. Before Ferguson turned around all three jars were already outside the spirit room.

'The figurehead, sir?' Hardy's heavy eyebrows lifted in innocent question. 'Oh, you mean Wally? I didn't know the Captain wanted to get rid of her.'

Ferguson nodded, his lips a tight line. His back was to Hardy again. 'Can't stand her, I'm afraid, Coxswain - thinks it's somewhat..eh...pansy for a fighting ship to be sporting a thing like that. Not good for morale. All right in peacetime, I suppose...' He turned to face the grinning coxswain. 'The Captain tried to have it removed officially but the C-in-C wouldn't hear of it. That's why the ...eh...operation would have to be completely unofficial. But I can assure you that Captain Taylor would be extremely grateful to you if you could arrange for its ...eh...disposal. Extremely grateful indeed.'

The clatter of boots on the iron ladder signalled the arrival of Leading Seaman Stevens and his work party. Coxswain Hardy winked solemnly at his superior officer. Ferguson recoiled inwardly from such unwelcome familiarity. He realised however that there was little he could do about it now that he had unburdened himself and his Captain to the coxswain.

'Tell the Captain not to give the matter another thought, sir,' Hardy whispered, lifting our four more empty jars from the deck and putting them outside. 'I'll attend to that matter right away...'

He turned to greet the work party. 'Right, Stevens, get that lot safely on the shelves and let's get these empties to the jetty. And warn Dusty to get a receipt for them. You can't trust those blood dockyard people with even an empty jar.'

By the time the stock of rum was stored and Lieutenant Ferguson had the spirit room locked, Coxswain Hardy had one full gallon jar of rum safely hidden in the cubby-hole under the f'xle that served as his office. He carried on out to the jetty where the last of the stores were being manhandled over the brow and ambled casually forward towards Manway's bow. Above him, Wally looked down, a smirk on her face, her jutting naked tits and cascading hair emphasizing the wanton appearance that so annoyed Captain Taylor.

Despite his assurance to Ferguson that the captain could leave everything safely to him as far as Wally's disposal was concerned, Hardy's heart sank when he studied the problem at close quarters. Definitely a dockyard job, he concluded ruefully. The bloody thing must have been firmly bolted and riveted to Manway's steel hull from the inside. No way could that brazen bitch be removed from the prow without massive internal surgery. He was surprised at Wally's buxom proportions under close inspection.

'Whether the old man likes you or not, you painted whore,' he whispered up to the figure-head, 'it looks like you're up there to stay.'

He was half way back to the brow when a sudden thought brought him to an abrupt halt. He went back to the bow and looked up again at Wally. A smile drifted across his face. Why oh why hadn't he seen that before? 'You're gone, Wally,' he whispered up to her. 'Discharged dead as from tonight. You won't be sailing with us tomorrow morning,' And he hurried back aboard, a satisfied feeling of achievement cheering him. A little tot of bubbly wouldn't go amiss, he thought. It's been a long day and there's a lot of work ahead of me tonight.'

In the stores a bewildered Supply Assistant O'Neill was wondering how half the contents of a carton of milk, two 7-lb tins of apple-and-plum jam and a quarter of a bag of sugar had gone missing between the brow and the store despite his unceasing vigilance. Tanky Blake was consoling him patiently when Coxswain Hardy arrived.

'Everything alright down here, Jack?' he asked O'Neill. The supply assistant looked at Tanky, unsure what to say.

'Not too bad, swain,' Tanky said philosophically. '12 tins of milk, two 7-lb tins of jam and a few pounds of sugar. I was just telling Jack here that it could be worse - it often was.'

Hardy shut the door and turned the key. His hand closed playfully on one cheek of O'Neill's backside bringing the hot colour rushing to his face as he recoiled from the unwelcome caress.

'Like Tanky said, Jack, it happens all the time. Didn't I tell you that you'd need eyes in your arse to watch a British matelot when you're taking on stores? But not to worry.' His grin was reassuring. 'All we have to do is give the bastards short measure till we get the stocks adjusted. They stole it from us - we give them short measure and take it back from them. That's how the system works. Tanky'll fix it in no time at all.' He turned to Tanky. 'Get the jar out old son, and we'll have a tot to make up for losing out on a good sleep. Bloody dockyard bastards, you'd think they'd know better than waking us up of an afternoon...'

O'Neill's eyes widened in shocked surprise when Tanky reached behind some sacks of sugar and lifted out a gallon jar of rum and a cup. Tanky extracted the cork, filled the cup with rum and handed it to Coxswain Hardy.

'Cheers,' Hardy said and grimaced when the fiery spirits hit his throat. He swallowed another mouthful and passed the cup to Tanky. Tanky gulped and a shudder rippled through him. He wiped his mouth and passed the cup to O'Neill. The supply assistant shook his head and pushed it away.

'For Christ's sake,' the coxswain said, 'I can understand you collecting the few pence a day in lieu of your tot of rum but if you're ever going to make it to Chief Petty Officer in this man's navy you'll have to learn how to handle your liquor.' He took the cup from Tanky and handed it to O'Neill. 'Go on, son, have a sipper. Now is as good a time as any to start.'

O'Neill hesitated, remembering what his mother had told him about the evils of alcohol. Then he gulped at the raw spirits. His tongue and throat went on fire and his belly heaved as he broke into a paroxysm of coughing. Hardy looked at what was left in the cup and drained it. Tanky was slapping O'Neill on the back. The coxswain grinned. 'You've a lot to learn yet about life in the navy - especially about life in the supply branch...' He fondled O'Neill's bottom affectionately. 'You'll be all right, Jack boy. Just let Tanky and me look after you.'

The duty officer had completed his night rounds when Coxswain Hardy looked into the lower deck recreation quarters. Because Manway was sailing at 07.00 hours and shore leave was restricted to 22.00 hours, most of the crew hadn't gone ashore. Some were playing darts, others writing letters. A noisy game of shove-ha'penny between two stokers who had just returned on board threatened to erupt into a fight. Tanky and Leading Seaman Stevens were seated on either side of O'Neill at the piano, their voices harmonizing unmusically in a strident rendition of Nelly Dean.

For men who hadn't been ashore, all three seemed to be in excellent form, the coxswain thought. The jar in the store had obviously been visited, and judging by O'Neill's flushed face he had overcome his initial dislike of navy rum. But keep it up lads, Hardy though, I have work to do and the more noise you make the better I like it.

On his way for'ard, he called at the Chief and Petty Officers' Mess to pick up his duffel coat. Petty Officer Joe Burgess looked up from the letter he was writing. He and the coxswain had served together on the Far East Station in the old days and were good mates. Now they liked to think that it was their combined experience and skills that kept Manway afloat despite the shortcomings off its Volunteer Reserve officers.

'Going ashore so late, Bert?' Burgess asked. 'Seems hardly worth while...' He tried not to show his concern but he had noticed that the coxswain was hitting the bottle a bit hard lately. Hardy put on his duffel coat.

'Just slipping down to the local for a pint or two,' he said lightly. 'Don't wait up for me.' Burgess sighed and got on with his letter.

The coxswain went for'ard to his office and collected the saw he had borrowed earlier from the bosun's stores. As an afterthought, he gave himself a good shot or rum to keep out the cold and climbed the ladder to the f'xle.

Black clouds clawed their way across the face of the moon and the breeze swirled around the blacked-out docks. Below him the cold waters of the Clyde lapped noisily at Manway's hull. Hardy mouthed a silent curse when his shin scraped roughly on a taut wire rope and he stumbled and nearly fell. Watch those fucking hawsers, Bert, he thought, or you'll be overboard. He groped his way to where Wally's head lifting above the line of the deck.

Carefully he placed the saw beside him and, stretching full length, he reached down as far as he could over the side. He grunted in satisfaction when, at last, his searching fingers closed over the cold fullness of Wally's right tit. He caressed it playfully for a second or two and then, pulling himself up into a sitting position, he attached the saw to his right wrist with a lanyard. He waited for a few seconds to check that the music was still loud from the recreation quarters. O'Neill, Tanky and Stevens were in excellent voice telling anybody who cared to listen that if one green bottle should accidentally fall, there'd be five green bottles hanging on the wall.

'Sorry about this, Wally you old whore,' he grunted into the dark. 'Just lie back and think of England and I promise you won't feel a thing.' Then with one gloved hand gripping the guardrail to prevent himself slipping overboard, he reached down and started sawing.

✥ ✥ ✥ ✥ ✥

Captain Taylor sat behind the small desk in his sea-cabin, his hands warming to the cup of tea the steward had brought him. Outside, the morning was still dark and he could feel the deck lifting and dropping gently under his feet. He was dressed in a roll-necked sweater and an old sea-going reefer jacket ready to face one more boring trip escorting a submarine down the Irish Sea to its patrol area in the Bay of Biscay. The tannoy had called out the special sea dutymen to their stations and ordered all watertight doors and scuttles to be secured. Lieutenant Ferguson would be arriving soon.

'Yes', he answered when the tap came on the door. Ferguson came into the cabin. 'Both parts of the watch ready for leaving harbour, sir. Starboard watch closed up at defence stations.' He cleared his throat and added, 'The coxswain hasn't returned on board from shore leave, I'm afraid, sir. According to Petty Officer Burgess, Hardy went ashore at 21.30 hours for a few pints and he hasn't returned on board.'

Captain Taylor gulped down the last of his tea, his eyes hardening. 'I'll have that bastard's guts for garters,' he said grimly. He put on his duffel coat and pulled his cap down tightly on his head. 'We'll have to get that man back to Portsmouth for his own good, Number One, before he finishes up being stripped down to ordinary seaman...'

Twenty minutes later, HMS Manway moved steadily out into the stream. Her bows lifted gently up and down as she burrowed into the grey waters of the Clyde, making it difficult for the lines of men on the forecastle and quarterdeck to hold steady.

The tannoy grated. 'Attention on the upper deck, face to port.' Captain Taylor saw the sleek outline of HMS Celbridge looming out of the morning mist, heading upstream. Celbridge, a town-class destroyer, shared the sub-escorting duties with Manway. She was commanded by Lieutenant Kirby, RN, a regular navy career officer who, taking his lead from the C-in-C, dismissed all reserve officers as 'bloody week-end sailors'.

The boson's whistle piped the salute as the two vessels passed. Out of the corner of his eye, Captain Taylor saw the signal lamp flashing from Celbridge.

On the forecastle, Lieutenant Ferguson also watched the winking lamp. 'Losing one's head in Glasgow could be deemed an accident,' he spelled out to himself. 'Losing one's tits as well seems downright careless.'

Ferguson's forehead tightened in perplexed lines. What on earth was Kirby at now? Then, hopeful curiosity welling inside him, but not sure what to expect, he moved right up for'ard. Grasping the guardrail, he leaned out and looked down. A delighted smile lit his cold face. 'Take charge here, Chief' he ordered Burgess brusquely. 'I must go to the bridge.'

Captain Taylor half turned in his chair to take the proffered signal-pad from Leading Signalman Jones. The signalman's puzzled expression was mirrored on Taylor's face when he read the signal from Celbridge.

'What the bloody...?' he started when Lieutenant Ferguson came dashing up the ladder to the bridge. Ferguson dismissed the signalman and grasped the captain's arm in his excitement.

'It's Wally, sir,' he gasped. Then realizing the extent of his familiarity, he released the captain's arm and pointed to the ship's bow. 'It must have been the coxswain, sir,' he whispered, recovering his composure. 'I asked him yesterday if he could do something about her - the figurehead, I mean, and now it doesn't look like - like a female anymore. In fact it doesn't look like anything other than a hunk of wood.' He paused uncertainly, at a loss for words. 'Her head's been cut off, sir and her tits. Sorry, sir, I mean her bosom...'

The tannoy intoned noisily. 'Attention on the upper deck. Face to port.' The boson's pipe returned the salute from the submarine awaiting Manway to escort her to the Bay.

The significance of Ferguson's report was slowly dawning on Captain Taylor. She was gone off his ship. He was free! The coxswain, somehow, had banished her forever. He knew that, at last, the submarine was saluting a fellow man-of-war, not that painted whore who had befouled his prow for so long. He came to attention on the bridge and proudly returned the salute.

'Make a signal to shore,' he ordered his First Lieutenant. 'Tell C-in-C that Coxswain Hardy was detained in Glasgow on ship's business and would he please arrange to have him travel on by rail to await our arrival in Plymouth.' He smacked the bridge rail with his gloved hand. 'By Christ,' he said aloud, 'I'll pin a medal on that man myself...'

✢ ✢ ✢ ✢ ✢

Beside the wall in Glasgow, the waters of the Clyde lapped at the wooden piles of the dock where HMS Manway had undergone her refit. A work party of dockers awaited the arrival of HMS Celbridge as she worked her way alongside the wall to occupy the berth recently vacated by Manway.

The churning waters spumed dirty white when Captain Kirby rang down to reverse the port engine. For a second or two, the duffel-coated body of Coxswain Hardy floated to the surface. The undercurrent caught it and sucked it under again. The handle of a saw attached to the coxswain's wrist snagged on an iron stud securing the wooden piles. The body was held firmly just below the surface, a shadowy blob in the darkness of the cold waters of the Clyde. For Coxswain Hardy the war was over.

CHAPTER TWO

THE BRISTOL CHANNEL

HMS Manway ploughed her way northwards through the choppy waters of the Irish Sea, bound once again for Glasgow. Lundy Isle loomed dimly on her starboard beam, its bulk lifting above the morning mist that cloaked the Bristol Channel.

'D'ye hear there?' intoned the ship's tannoy .'Up spirits.'

Supply Assistant O'Neill and Tanky Blake took last drags on their cigarettes in the storeroom before stubbing out the butts in the lid of a tobacco tin that served as an ashtray.

'You sure you've got everything right, Tanky?' O'Neill asked, pointing at the brass rum measures ranging from one gallon down to an eight of a pint. Tanky nodded impatiently.

Since the signal reached the ship, six months before, that Coxswain Hardy was dead, Tanky Blake had taken on the chore of nursing and guiding the inexperienced O'Neill. The complicated guidelines of King's Rules and Admiralty Instructions, and the tricks and dodges that made for the victualling of the crew of any of His Majesty's men-of-war was at last becoming clearer to O'Neill.

Today was the last day of the month and Midshipman Davies, the duty officer, had told O'Neill that he intended to stock-take in the spirit room. Tanky shook the gallon measure and O'Neill could hear the water swirling around inside it.

'I've smuggled four tots of water into the Spirit Room every day for the last five weeks and the three tots I've in there now should bring the stock bang on.' He twirled the gallon measure around reassuringly. 'There's no pink-arsed snotty in this man's navy going to catch me out. As long as you're sure your figures are right in the books, then we've fuck-all to worry about.'

The solemn routine of getting up spirits from the spirit room and dispensing the requisite ration to the various messes was a ceremony dating back to Nelson's days.

The Spirit Book showing the amount of rum to be issued to each mess was prepared by the supply assistant. Punishment stoppages ordered by the Captain or the Number One were passed on to him by the Coxswain.

When 'Up Spirits' was piped at seven bells in the forenoon watch, the supply assistant reported to the duty officer. Then they and the duty petty officer gathered at the spirit room.

'The Chiefs and Petty Officers get their rum ration neat,' Tanky had explained to O'Neill. 'I'll measure out the rum for the remaining messes into this measure and that's how I get the few tots of water in to it. Then we bring it all up to the quarter-deck.'

There, an oak tub, bound in hoops of brass and bearing the legend 'God save the King' was used for dispensing the rations to the messes.

The neat rum was poured into the tub and then twice as much water was liberally added. The Senior Rating from each mess collected his mess's ration. This mixture, know as grog, had to be consumed immediately and not kept for later use because the added water soon made it flat and unpalatable.

When the issue was completed, the surplus grog was brought back to the Victualling Office and poured down the sink in the presence of the duty officer. An alert tanky would always manage to get the stopper into the sink before too much of the surplus drained away. The Victualling office staff then consumed what he saved.

'Right then, Jack,' Tanky snapped impatiently, 'up to the bridge with you and report to the duty officer. I'll be waiting at the spirit room.'

O'Neill paused at the bottom of the ladder leading to the bridge and sucked in deep breaths of the cold Bristol Channel air to clear his head for the ordeal ahead. The staccato chatter of machine-gun fire suddenly shattered the silence. He looked around in surprise. Behind him, on the ship's starboard quarter, the grey waters erupted in a line of smacking splashes. They stretched from a point just abreast the bridge and moved steadily away from the ship.

O'Neill watched, fascinated, wondering what Manway's gunners could be firing at. He ducked in fright when an aeroplane zoomed above the ship at masthead height, the roar of its engines and chattering machine-guns tearing at his eardrums. When it veered off, gaining height, he saw the black crosses painted on its wings and sides.

'Jesus!' His stomach turned over. 'We're being attacked by a Jerry.' He scrambled up the ladder, taking every second rung in his terror and made it to the bridge wing.

'We're being attacked...' he babbled. Then his voice broke off in horror.

Leading Seaman Tom Stevens's body was slumped under the Oerlikon machine-gun mounting, the twin barrels pointing futilely at the grey sky. Blood spurted from a gaping wound in his stomach which had almost cut him in two. O'Neill felt his own stomach heave. He had never seen a dead body before.

Inside the open bridge, the screen was shattered and glass splinters littered the deck. The woodwork was pocked and torn where the plane's cannon shells had ripped into it. Midshipman Cliff Davies lay on his back on the grating, his open eyes staring unseeingly, his face twisted in agony and surprise. The riddled bodies of the signalman and the lookout on the port wing were slumped in heaps, rivulets of blood oozing along the deck from their torn bodies. O'Neill felt the bile rising in his dry throat. 'Jesus,' he said again and vomited.

Sub-Lieutenant Gordon was clinging to the gyrocompass, his eyes staring, blood oozing from the corners of his mouth. He saw O'Neill and tried to speak, gesticulating frantically with his free hand at the red alarm button which would sound off the Action Station bells. O'Neill forced himself to control the trembling which was shaking his body.

'I get you, sir...' he heard himself gasp. O'Neill pressed the button and the alarm bells echoed through the ship. Sub-Lieutenant Gordon, his duty done, slumped into a sitting position and died, his head resting against the bulkhead.

The captain had left the bridge just a minute before to fetch his pipe from the sea cabin. Sub-Lieutenant Gordon had the forenoon watch and was checking his charts. Midshipman Davies was standing beside him waiting for the supply assistant to report that he was ready to get up spirits.

The signalman and two lookouts, aware that the captain had left the bridge, allowed their concentration to relax. After all, there was nothing out there but the horizon and the dark outline of Lundy Isle. Everything was perfectly normal, just another routine trip from Plymouth to Glasgow. It was their fifteenth such mission without experiencing trouble.

Captain Taylor had taken the pipe from the rack on the bulkhead when the light steel partition, which separated the chart-house from his sea cabin, disintegrated in an uneven pattern of punctured holes. He was flung heavily against the desk before slumping onto the deck. Black waves of unconsciousness swept over him. His searching hand found the wound that was his smashed right shoulder. Vaguely he heard the roar of the plane zooming over the bridge as he pulled himself up into a sitting position. Then, grasping the edge of the desk, he struggled to his feet. Unsteadily, he groped his way forward along the walkway to the open bridge.

Relief flooded through O'Neill when he saw the captain, to be replaced by despair and panic when he saw the blood oozing from the gaping wound in his shoulder.

'We're being attacked, sir,' he stuttered, 'a Jerry plane...'

The captain staggered. O'Neill grabbed him by the elbow and helped him to the tall chair, which was bolted to the deck behind the now shattered glass screens.

'Cox'n on the wheel, sir,' came the tones of Coxswain Sherlock from the wheelhouse voice-pipe. Sherlock, a navy regular from Cardiff, had replaced Coxswain Bert Hardy. In total contrast, he was a teetotaller and rarely bothered to go ashore, preferring to spend his off-duty hours reading. The collected works of Dickens held pride of place on a shelf above his locker in the Chiefs' mess.

'Quartermaster Jones was slightly injured in that attack,' he reported calmly, 'but he'll be okay...'

Captain Taylor leaned forward to the voice-pipe, and nearly fell off the chair. O'Neill grabbed at him and held him erect. A strangled moan drowned in the captain's throat. O'Neill felt the oozing blood under his restraining hand and his stomach heaved again.

'Get hold of yourself, man,' Taylor gasped 'I need you now...' The pain-filled eyes held O'Neill's in a steady stare. 'Tell the coxswain to steer three-five-zero and hold it steady.'

O'Neill put his mouth to the wheelhouse voice-pipe.

'Steer three-five-zero, cox'n,' he ordered, 'and hold it steady.' He felt the ship bracing as the coxswain applied the correcting steerage.

'Steering three-five-zero, sir' confirmed Sherlock, and then unable to contain his curiosity, 'Who - who's this...?' And to cover himself in case he was showing disrespect, he added 'sir.'

'Supply Assistant O'Neill, cox'n.' There was a long silence.

'Bloody, bleedin' hell...!' There was no doubting that as far as Coxswain Sherlock was concerned, HMS Manway and her crew were in a bad way.

Captain Taylor grimaced, indicating the handset connected to the quarterdeck. 'Ask Lieutenant Ferguson to get up here right away,' he whispered hoarsely.

O'Neill had to move the midshipman's body to reach the handset. He recognised Lieutenant's Ferguson's voice immediately. The First Lieutenant had been standing anxiously by the phone wondering what was happening on the bridge.

'Supply Assistant O'Neill, sir!' He heard the lieutenant's startled intake of breath. 'Captain says for you to report to the bridge right away, sir.' Then he gasped out, 'And tell the sick berth attendant to get up here as well and hurry, sir, please. They're all cut to bits...'

The four-inch gun on the quarterdeck was being brought to bear on the distant outline of the German plane as it turned to make another attacking run. Hearing the pounding bangs, O'Neill picked his way over the bodies littering the deck and scrambled to the port bridge wing to see what was happening.

The sun caught the distant silhouette of the plane, picking it out clearly in the lifting mist. It was about three miles away on the port quarter and closing fast. Black puffy splashes marked the explosions of Manway's shells around it.

'Get down, sir, for God's sake,' he shouted to the captain. 'He's coming at us again from...' His mind couldn't grapple with the complexity of naval terms for left and right and the back and front of the ship. 'He's coming at us from the left side at the back...'

Captain Taylor pushed him away and leaned over the wheelhouse voice-pipe. 'Sta'board ten, cox'n,' he ordered. If O'Neill's reading of the direction from which the attack was being pressed was correct he wanted to present the narrowest possible target to the enemy plane.

'Sta'board ten, it is, sir.' The relief in Sherlock's voice made him sound almost jubilant as he realised that O'Neill wasn't, after all, in sole command of Manway.

Out of the corner of his eye, O'Neill saw that Tom Steven's body was still twitching spasmodically in the last throes of death. Cold anger welled up inside him. You bastards, he thought, you bloody German bastards. He lifted the body by the elbows and pulled it into the shelter of the bridge.

In a ten-minute gunnery lecture at Whale Island, during his training period, a taciturn three-badge gunner's mate had given the class of trainee supply assistants a demonstration in the art of aiming and firing an Oerlikon.

'You gets the target in your sights as so,' he told them in a bored Geordie accent, aiming casually at a sea-gull floating high above the Solent, two hundred yards away, 'and you presses the firing button as so...'

One shot rang out. To the astonished awe of the twenty supply ratings, the unfortunate sea gull exploded in a tattered mess of flying feathers and tumbled down into the sea. The gunner's mate, as surprised as his pupils, didn't even blink.

'There's fuck-all to it when you knows what you're at,' he told them. 'Any questions?'

O'Neill heard the distant rattle of the plane's machine-guns and cannon mingling discordantly with the intermittent bangs of Manway's four-inch gun. His stomach tightened. From the age of ten, he had spent most winter weekends shooting pheasants on his Uncle Eugene's farm in Ireland.

'Don't aim your gun at the spot where the dog is pointing,' Eugene had instructed his nephew, 'or you'll never get a bird. Always aim about twelve feet above him and when the pheasant jumps, at least your gun will be pointing generally in the right direction. When he comes into your sights, give him everything you've got.'

O'Neill braced himself behind the Oerlikon. Turning his back to the oncoming fighter he aimed the twin barrels out over the ship's prow where Wally had once sat in isolated grandeur. His exposed back cringed when he heard the bullets and shells smash into the funnel above him. He saw the deck of the f'xle gouge open in long strips. Then, just like the escaping pheasant, the sleek silver body of the plane swept into his sights. It climbed obligingly and exposed its bulging underbelly.

O'Neill's sweaty thumbs pressed the firing buttons, bringing the heavy Oerlikon to life. Long probing balls of tracer reached out and raked the plane from stem to stern. As it twisted and turned in the air, the curving tracers followed in bloodthirsty chase, holding, holding, holding...

The explosion blinded O'Neill. One moment the plane was there, trying desperately to escape from his sights. Next it shattered into a black cloud of smoke and flame, hung in the sky. Then it exploded and tumbled headlong into the waters of the Irish Sea.

'Good show, O'Neill!' Lieutenant Ferguson's voice was unemotional, trying to conceal the panic that engulfed him when he saw the carnage on the battered bridge.

O'Neill had been unaware of the activity around him. The sick berth attendant, having confirmed that all the bridge party caught in the first attack were dead, was helping Captain Taylor along the walkway to his sea cabin. His helpers were manhandling the bodies down the bridge ladders to place them in a bloody row on the quarterdeck.

Captain Taylor paused beside the Oerlikon mounting and reached out his left hand to the sweating supply assistant.

'Thank you, son,' he said. 'I'll be recommending you for a decoration for your conduct under fire...'

O'Neill looked down at Tom Steven's twisted body lying at his feet, the oozing blood staining his shoes. The Spirit Book which he had dropped in his panic when he came on the bridge - it seemed as if it had been hours before - was lying beside him. O'Neill picked it up, still in a daze, and looked across at the body of Midshipman Davies who was supposed to supervise the day's spirit issue. He felt his stomach turn again.

'D'ye hear there?' Lieutenant Ferguson had the tannoy microphone to his mouth. He had just realised that, with a badly wounded captain, he was not only the senior officer, he was the only functioning executive officer on the Manway.

'Secure from action stations,' he ordered. 'Sta'board watch close up at defence stations. Petty Officer Burgess report to the bridge immediately.' He leaned forward to the wheelhouse voice-pipe. 'Steady as she goes, coxswain. And report up here as soon as you're relieved on the wheel. We have to do some reorganizing of the ship's company after that little to-do.' He turned to O'Neill. 'You'll have to get up spirits on your own, O'Neill,' he told him. 'I can't spare anybody to supervise it. And see to it that everything is done properly.' His lips relaxed in a congratulatory smile. 'I know you don't touch the stuff yourself but I think it would be quite in order to give yourself a tot today. You look like you need one, and you certainly deserve it.'

Tanky Blake was waiting impatiently for O'Neill in the store. He had already given himself a bolstering tot from the jar behind the bags of sugar.

'Is it true 'twas you what shot down the Jerry?' he asked. O'Neill, his face pale and his hands still trembling, nodded in embarrassment. Tanky banged him on the back

'Jesus, Jack lad,' he grinned happily, 'that makes you a fucking hero! And because you're my winger we'll never have to buy a drink again as long as we're aboard this tub.' He poured a brimming tot of rum into the cup and handed it to O'Neill. 'How the fuck did you do it?'

O'Neill threw back the rum in a quick gulp, coughed and grimaced. He forced a grin. 'There's fuck-all to it,' he said, 'when you knows what you're at.'

'Right,' said Tanky, gathering the spirit measures together, 'we'd better get the bubbly up. The whole ship's company's gasping for a drink.' He paused uncertainly. 'I take it the fucking stock-take is off?'

O'Neill nodded. 'But there's just one thing I have to check out before we get up spirits.' He hurried off, a puzzled Tanky following behind. When they got to the recreation quarters, O'Neill went in and headed straight for the piano.

'Jesus, Jack,' said Tanky, 'you're not going playing that fucking thing now...'.

O'Neill examined the Steinway carefully, checking for any signs of damage. At last, he straightened up, smiling happily.

'Not a scratch,' he whispered. 'Not a fucking scratch.' He kissed the lid of the piano. 'You're a beauty, sweetheart, that's what you are, a fucking beauty' He turned to Tanky. 'Okay, me old mate, let's get the bubbly up...'

✛ ✛ ✛ ✛ ✛

HMS Manway, now bloodied and scarred from her first victorious encounter with the enemy was tied to the wall in Fishguard. Captain Taylor had been taken to hospital and the word filtered back that he'd not be going to sea again.

Manway's newly promoted captain, Lieutenant-Commander Ferguson, RNVR, stood on the bridge and ran a surreptitious finger proudly over the extra half stripe on his sleeve. The dead had been buried with full naval honours and Ferguson had written the necessary letters to the relatives. Replacements for the officers and ratings killed in the encounter with the German plane were due on board tomorrow and his orders were to proceed to Glasgow for repairs.

O'Neill was supervising the loading of potatoes at the forward brow. Out of the corner of his eye he could see the new captain pacing up and down the bridge.

'Three bags is the most we can risk,' Tanky whispered to him, 'We're still two bags down from the last lot and that means we'll have to make up five bags over the next few months.' He nodded in the direction of the lorry driver. 'We've taken on 37 bags now so sign for the two ton and get a couple of quid off him - and make sure the old man don't spot you getting paid off.'

O'Neill was now getting accustomed to the wheeling and dealing that went on, the world over, between supply ratings and contractors who supplied goods to the Royal Navy. However, his heart still beat a little nervously when he became directly involved in such underhand deals.

Along with sex, O'Neill had been constantly lectured in school about the consequences of the sin of theft. He had been warned repeatedly that one would have to do years of suffering in purgatory if compensation for stolen goods wasn't made before one died. O'Neill wondered how many thousands of years of suffering would three bags of spuds cost? He shrugged and consoled himself with the thought that the transaction would just about finance a couple of runs ashore for himself and Tanky.

After 'Up Spirits' Tanky seemed reluctant to take a drink from the leftover grog in the Victualling office sink. O'Neill looked at him in surprise. Now a fairly hardened tippler himself, he had never known Tanky to refuse before.

'You okay?' he asked, hiccuping slightly as he topped up the quarter pint measure he was using as a glass. 'You'll be okay for a run ashore tonight, won't you?' He patted the pocket that held the money given to him by the contractor. 'We've got the few bob and this'll be our last chance to try the Fishguard bints.'

When O'Neill and Tanky went ashore in search of romance, O'Neill was still the shy one and he depended on his more experienced mate to make the running with the girls. He watched Tanky's face anxiously when there was no reply to his invitation. 'You sure you're okay, Tanky?'

Tanky bit on his lower lip and then smacked his clinched fist into the palm of his hand. 'Okay, Jack, fill me out a noggin,' he nodded, pointing to the sink, 'I might as well have me a last fling.'

O'Neill handed him the brimming measure. 'Last fling?' he asked, puzzled. 'What gives with you, for Chris' sake.'

Tanky gulped at the measure and shuddered. 'Those two bints we picked up in Plymouth,' he said at last, 'did you by any chance get to dip your wick with your bit?'

O'Neill coloured and shook his head, busying himself storing away the empty rum measures.

Tanky grunted. 'You're bloody lucky then, Jack.' He heaved a big sigh and emptied the last of the grog down his throat. The half-pint measure rattled noisily into the empty sink. 'I think I've got me a tear...'

O'Neill's forehead wrinkled as he looked at Tanky's eyes. 'A tear?' he asked. 'I don't see any tears.'

'Jesus, Jack,' Tanky groaned, 'don't you know any fucking thing at all? A tear. A dose. The pox. I'll have to report sick. For the last couple of days every time I go to the heads it's like pissing broken glass and fish-hooks. I'll be bloody lucky if it's only a tear...'

Tanky went to the local hospital next day and it was confirmed that he had contracted gonorrhoea. Captain Ferguson was in his day cabin when Coxswain Sherlock reported that three officers and four ratings had joined the ship.

'Thanks, coxswain.' He nodded. 'Have the steward show the officers their cabins and tell them that I'll join them in the Wardroom shortly. You'll allocate the ratings to their messes.' He looked up at the waiting coxswain. 'Did you say four ratings? Surely we only requested three?'

Sherlock checked his clipboard. 'There's a Leading Supply Assistant McGregor sir - he's the extra hand. Don't know why...' He hesitated and then added, 'by strange coincidence, sir, Able Seaman Blake has gone down sick and he's been sent to hospital - a dose, I'm afraid, sir. So with the extra Jack Dusty we won't need to replace the tanky for the moment, I understand Blake will be back in about ten days.'

Leading Supply Assistant McGregor had already introduced himself to the surprised O'Neill in the victualling office. A small weedy man with a Scottish accent, he looked no more than a year or so older than O'Neill but he soon made it quite clear that he was the senior hand and was now in charge.

'I'll take over the keys of the storerooms and we'll do a stock-take this afternoon,' he informed O'Neill. He looked around the cramped victualling office. 'And get your gear out of here,' he ordered brusquely. 'There's not room for the both of us in here.'

The stock-take was going badly and O'Neill was getting more and more depressed as the afternoon wore on. Nearly everything they checked seemed to be short - the list ranged through tinned milk, tea, jam, baked beans...

'I don't believe this, 'McGregor told his junior grimly as he looked down the growing list of stock deficiencies. They had just returned to the stores after stand-easy and a cup of tea. 'What the hell have ye been at? When did ye check the stocks last?'

O'Neill tried to explain that he had left all that sort of thing to Tanky Blake. It was then that McGregor pulled aside a bag of sugar and the wickerwork jar and the cup rolled out on the deck. He picked up the jar in disbelief, his eyes wide. O'Neill felt his legs go weak. If ever he needed a drink, he needed one now. The one thing that both Coxswain Hardy and Tanky had constantly drummed into him was that getting caught fiddling the sailors' rum was, in the eyes of the Lords of the Admiralty, the most heinous crime of all.

McGregor slowly extracted the cork and sniffed, his lips set in a tight line. 'This is rum,' he confirmed, his voice accusing, each word damning as if he could already hear the captain reading out the Articles of War before pronouncing sentence on the quaking O'Neill. He rattled the jar and established that it was half full, then replaced the cork.

'You're for the high jump for this little lot, O'Neill.' His voice was brimming with indignant righteousness. 'I'm beginning to understand now why the stocks are in the mess they're in. D'ye spend yer day on the piss or what?'

✧ ✧ ✧ ✧ ✧

HMS Manway was back for repairs at the berth in Glasgow docks where the unfortunate Coxswain Hardy had drowned just six months before. Coxswain Sherlock brought Leading Supply Assistant McGregor and Supply Assistant O'Neill to the Captain's cabin. The coxswain had already outlined to Ferguson the results of the stock-take. Now the captain's gaze ran down the list of stock deficiencies, which McGregor had presented to him.

'What have you to say for yourself, O'Neill?' he asked at last.

O'Neill swallowed nervously and shook his head. 'Nothing, sir, I'm afraid. I suppose I just didn't know what I was at.'

Captain Ferguson nodded. That was exactly what he thought, and he was very conscious of the fact that such a state of affairs wasn't fully O'Neill's fault. In this bloody war, both officers and ratings with inadequate training were constantly being thrown into situations which they were quite incapable of handling. And men were dying because of it.

He recalled only too clearly the day the German plane had slipped up on them unnoticed. They could just as easily have lost the ship because some of the officers and ratings, like O'Neill, quite obviously didn't know what they were at. And he had been the Number One responsible for the fighting efficiency of the ship's company.

He shook his head slowly, studying the list. He knew that Captain Taylor had recommended O'Neill for a decoration for bravery but this turn of events would certainly put a stop to that.

'At least the rum stock is alright,' Ferguson said at last. He looked up at O'Neill. 'You can be thankful for that. Otherwise I'd come down on you like a ton of bricks.'

O'Neill avoided his eyes. Thanks be to God, he thought, Tanky had managed to square off the rum stock before he went to hospital. Given another month or so, they'd have got the whole thing right.

The captain looked at McGregor. He knew he was being totally unfair to him but he had taken an instant dislike to the man.

'Alright, you two,' he barked, scowling at the two supply ratings. 'I'll give this matter some thought and then I'll decide what has to be done.' He turned to McGregor. 'By the way, what sort of a - a rig was that I saw you wearing on the jetty this morning?'

McGregor smiled brightly. 'That's my shop coat, sir,' he told him. 'I was a shop assistant in a grocery store before I was called up and I still use the coat. After all, sir, as far as I'm concerned, working aboard a ship like this is no different from working in a grocery store.'

Captain Ferguson's eyebrows shot up and he turned abruptly to the coxswain. 'I'll be obliged, cox'n, if you see to it in future that all hands dress in the rig of the day in accordance with Daily Orders.' He dismissed the two supply ratings.

Coxswain Sherlock sensed that it was his turn now to get a bottle about lax shipboard discipline. Because the new First Lieutenant was a regular navy officer, he could see that the newly-promoted Volunteer Reserve skipper wasn't going to tolerate anything that might give rise to criticism of the way he ran his ship.

'Sit down, cox'n,' Ferguson said wearily, 'and help me decide what we're to do about this bloody fool, O'Neill. After all, he was the only one who kept his wits about him when the Jerry plane caught the rest of us with our trousers around our ankles.'

He stood for fully a minute staring out of the open porthole in silence. His face twisted in a smile when he turned around and sensed Sherlock's obvious unease. 'Tell me, cox'n,' he asked at last. 'Do you ever get the uneasy feeling that maybe McGregor is right and that this damned ship that I'm so proud to command is nothing more than a fucking floating grocery store?'

Captain Ferguson had gone through the solemn routine of reading the Articles of War to the assembled ship's company of HMS Manway. Then he pronouncing sentence of five days detention on Supply Assistant O'Neill for failing in his duty to keep accurate and proper account of His Majesty's stores. He had agreed with Coxswain Sherlock that it was essential for the maintenance of good order and discipline that some charges should be brought against O'Neill. This was as easy as he could go on him.

'On cap! Right turn,' Coxswain Sherlock ordered O'Neill after sentence was pronounced. The hapless supply assistant was marched away under escort to serve his sentence on board HMS Lucan, an armed merchant cruiser undergoing refit in the next dock. HMS Manway was due to resume her escorting duties at 17.00 hours.

Lieutenant James, RN, the new Number One, was on the bridge when the captain joined him.

'Have we finally got rid of those damned dockyard mateys, Number One?' Ferguson asked, looking around the refurbished bridge. James was standing by the starboard wing platform looking down on the jetty. He turned with a start when he heard the captain.

'Sorry, sir,' he apologised quickly, 'I - I was..' He pointed down the jetty. 'Did you ever see anything like that carry-on, sir, in all your naval career?' he blurted out. There was shocked amazement in his voice. Ferguson joined him at the rail. Supply Assistant O'Neill with an escort of two of Manway's able seamen wearing Naval Police armlets, had gone over the for'ard brow and were marching in line abreast along the jetty to where HMS Lucan was moored. One of the escort was carrying O'Neill's hammock and attache case and the other was shouldering his kit-bag.

'The escort are actually carrying the prisoner's gear for him. Who the bloody hell's supposed to be escorting whom...?'

They heard Coxswain Sherlock's barked order dismissing the ship's company still assembled on the f'xle. Immediately there was an undisciplined rush to the starboard rail and sporadic cheering broke out. O'Neill and his escort stopped and looked back.

'For O'Neill's a jolly good fellow, O'Neill's a jolly good fellow, O'Neill's a jolly good fellow and so say all of us...' The inharmonious chorus echoed through the dockyard. The entire ship's company waved their caps in the air, cheering. Captain Ferguson suppressed a smile when he saw O'Neill clasp his two hands above his head in waving acknowledgement of his shipmates' farewell. Then O'Neill and his escort marched away.

Lieutenant James shook his head. What else could one expect in a ship commanded by a bloody week-end sailor, he thought. Obviously he was going to have his work cut out whipping this motley crew into some sort of a disciplined fighting force.

Captain Ferguson knew that the lieutenant's father was a captain and his grandfather an admiral and the family probably stretched back to Nelson's day. He could sense what was passing through the regular navy officer's mind and was surprised to find that he no longer resented it.

Coxswain Sherlock came on to the bridge and saluted. 'O'Neill asked me to give you this, sir,' he said and handed the captain a small key. Captain

Ferguson looked at it and then turned to Lieutenant James, a smile twisting his mouth.

'Now that O'Neill is no longer with us,' he said, 'I'm afraid that this will have to be one more of your responsibilities, Number One.' He handed the key to the lieutenant who stared at it uncomprehendingly.

'It's the key of our grand piano,' Ferguson explained. 'It's a Steinway, don't you know... a truly magnificent instrument.'

HMS Manway was, once again, fully fitted and ready for war.

Chapter Three

Portsmouth

Nothing much had changed in Portsmouth during the seven months O'Neill had been at sea. HMS Conway was one of several barracks where rooky sailors were trained, like Britannia, to rule the waves. Its buildings, smoke-blacked and weather-beaten over the years, towered around the sprawling parade-ground. Apoplectic gunner's mates shouted orders at squads of trainee sailors marching untidily up and down, backwards and forwards, forming fours, dressing left or right, fixing and unfixing their bayonets. Everywhere, sailors wandered around with bits of paper in their hands seeking endless rubber-stamps. Naval routine, war or no war, went on as usual.

The first morning aboard Conway, O'Neill woke up to the clatter of plates and dishes. He lifted himself up in his hammock and peered drowsily over the side. When he slung the hammock the night before, the mess was empty. Now there were people everywhere. A line of supply ratings, all still dressed in the overcoats and caps they had worn ashore, were queuing to collect their breakfast from the mess cooks. Others wolfed down their food at the tables beneath him. They were obviously barrack staff who lived ashore with their families but were victualled in the barracks. O'Neill flopped back in his hammock, panic mounting inside him.

After he joined HMS Manway he had soon lapsed into the habit of all lower deck personnel of either sleeping stark naked or, at the most, wearing only their underpants. His hand slipped down under the blanket and pushed his piss-proud penis back inside his underpants. Jesus, he thought miserably, his face and neck burning, how am I going to get out of the hammock in front of this shower?

He lifted his head cautiously to check where his clothes were. When he undressed the night before he had folded each item neatly and placed them on the nearby table. There were four supply ratings eating at that table and one of them must have moved his clothes which were now on top of a locker ten feet away.

O'Neill's gaze met those of the occupant of the only other hammock slung in the mess. He too was looking about him in sleepy surprise. O'Neill watched him furtively as he brushed back his dark curly hair with his hand. Then, quite unconcerned, he lifted himself out of the hammock and dropped lightly to the deck. O'Neill's eyes popped. The man was bollick naked and nobody was taking any notice.

O'Neill checked once more to make sure his own private parts were safely covered in his underpants and then he too lifted himself out of the hammock. He grabbed his clothes from the top of the locker, pulled on his trousers and headed for the bathroom, his face burning in embarrassment.

He met up again with Supply Assistant George Hoskins in the Regulating Office, also going through the joining-ship routine. Together they spent the next two days leisurely queuing to have their bodies viewed and prodded, to cough on command, and to be examined and cross-examined by medical officers, dental officers, paymasters and a host of other minor officials, all of whom duly stamped their chits.

This chore successfully completed, Supply Assistant James O'Neill, Roman Catholic, and Supply Assistant George Hoskins, Church of England, once again became part of the crew of HMS Conway. From now until such time as they were drafted to a new ship, they would be fed three meals a day, get their rum ration, a monthly supply of duty-free cigarettes and, of course, their pay - three shillings and six pence per day.

They were ordered by their Divisional Officer, a harassed Paymaster Lieutenant, to report for duty to the Supply Chief Petty Officer in charge of the clothing stores.

'How does that bloody imbecile think I can find work for every shagger that passes through these barracks?' Supply Chief Petty Officer Hall demanded when they presented themselves for duty at 08.30 hours.

Hoskins was a veteran of nearly three years destroyer service in peace and war. He had made four runs to Dunkirk and was one of only 20 survivors when the destroyer finally ran out of luck and hit a magnetic mine at the entrance to Portsmouth harbour. He'd been through this routine before.

'Not to worry, Chief,' he said brightly. 'We've both volunteered for sea duty as soon as possible so we won't be bothering you for too long in this kip.'

The Paymaster Lieutenant had given the Chief a run-down on Hoskins's war record to date, with emphasis on the fact that when the destroyer was sunk, Hoskins had supported an injured officer in the water for over three hours until they were picked up by a searching MTB.

As for O'Neill, the captain of HMS Manway had discreetly omitted to make any mention on the record sheet of his misdemeanours and the consequent five-day incarceration in cells. He had, however, commented at length on his bravery, above and beyond the call of duty, in single handedly shooting down an attacking Messerschmitt and possibly saving the ship and the lives of many of its crew. That, he felt, compensated somewhat for the fact that O'Neill had missed out on, at least, an MBE.

Chief Hall wasn't impressed. He and his permanent staff had handy numbers here in Conway and they were all living with their families in Portsmouth. Their war was a nine to five job and they didn't want their cosy domestic routines endangered by stupid bloody heroes like these two.

'Don't give me any of your smart-ass lip, sonny-boy,' he snorted at Hoskins. He pointed to the ladder leading to the overhead warehouse where the clothing was kept in unopened bales and boxes. 'Up aloft with the both of you. There's a couple of sprogs under-employed there already but there's fuckall else for you to do around here.' He paused and wagged a finger at them. 'You take charge, Hoskins, being the senior hand, and make bloody sure that nothing is opened before it comes down the chute to the main store. Okay? I'll have no bloody fiddling in my slop room.'

'Aye, aye, Chief,' Hoskins answered cheerily. 'Not to worry. I know what I'm at...' O'Neill grimaced but and he kept a discreet silence. He may have been caught out once but by now he hoped that he too knew what he was at. He didn't intend to get caught again.

Hoskins had worked in the clothing store in HMS Victory before his first draft to sea so the slop room routine wasn't new to him. Unlike the army and air force, naval ratings, after their initial kitting-out, were paid a weekly allowance to maintain their kit.

The slop room opened like any draper's shop at certain hours. A rating wishing to buy clothes filled out a slop chit listing his name, official number and the items required. The supply assistant behind the counter priced the items, took the customer's money, and handed out the clothes. The routine was, in fact, little different to that of any draper's shop ashore except for one obvious fact - the prices of clothing items in His Majesty's slop rooms were about a tenth of the prices paid for similar articles ashore. To supply staff with vision, this fact opened up vistas undreamt of in the drapery trade.

Hoskins introduced himself and O'Neill to the two supply assistants already working in the loft warehouse and made it clear to all that, as from now, he was in charge. A trap-door in the floor was connected to the slop room below by a wooden chute. When a box or bale of clothing was required in the slop room, the Chief shouted up the order to Hoskins, who arranged for his three-man crew to locate it in the warehouse, man-handle it to the trap-door and slide it down the chute.

When the two juniors were dispatched to their stand-easy tea-break, Hoskins quickly established with O'Neill where the white shirts worn by chiefs and petty officers were stored.

'Size 16 is a popular size,' he told O'Neill. According to the code mark, the bale he finally selected contained 200 shirts, all size 16. Together they pulled and hauled until they got it to a rack which, according to the code markings, held arctic underwear.

'What the hell are we at?' O'Neill asked breathlessly. He blinked in surprise when he saw Hoskins carefully unpicking the twine with which the bale had been sewn.

Hoskins winked. 'Beer money!' He had loosened enough of the seam to be able to extract ten shirts. Then he pulled on the loosened string and secured the packet again.

'For Chris' sake, Paddy, don't just stand there with your mouth open, will you?' he whispered urgently. 'Help me get this fucking lot turned inwards so that the split and the code mark don't show.' O'Neill tugged and hauled with him until they got the shirts stowed at the back of the rack behind the packets of arctic underwear.

'It'll be months before they'll need arctic underwear down below,' Hoskins whispered, 'if they ever need it. By then you and I will be well out of this place.' He handed O'Neill five of the shirts. 'Hide your gas-mask in there.' He had already opened his own gas-mask bag and hidden the mask at the back of the rack. He then folded the five shirts into the empty bag. He gestured impatiently to O'Neill. 'Chop, chop for God's sake, Paddy,' he told him. 'We don't want those two sprogs to see what we're at.'

O'Neill's heart was thudding uncomfortably when he and Hoskins lined up for inspection with the liberty men at 16.30 hours. Apart from seeing to it that all ratings going ashore were dressed properly, shoes polished, caps set squarely on the head, gas-mask over the left shoulder, the Duty Regulating Petty Officer was also supposed to ensure that nobody breached navy regulations by carrying more that 20 duty-free cigarettes ashore. Hoskins nudged O'Neill.

'Not to worry, Paddy,' he whispered, 'even if he does search you, he's too fucking thick to think of checking the gas-mask..'

The Regulating Petty Officer didn't bother to check anybody or anything. He brought the liberty men to attention and gave the order to carry on ashore.

Commercial Road was the narrow overcrowded main artery that stretched from Portsmouth's imposing Town Hall right through the centre of the city. It was a snaking length of street with so many bars it was claimed that nobody could drink a mouthful of beer in each of them and be still standing when he reached the last.

Hoskins and O'Neill headed for Aggie Weston's, a hostel for sailors, where they booked two cabins for the night. They then partook of beans and toast in the basement cafe. O'Neill looked furtively around the cafe crowded with sailors all intent on laying down a solid food foundation for the long night ahead. He tapped the gas-mask bag surreptitiously.

'What will we do with...you know what?' he asked, feeling more daring now that they were safely ashore with the booty.

George Hoskins winked, his mouth full of beans and toast. 'Not to worry, Paddy,' he whispered, 'I have a contact - an ex officer's steward, Ernie Richards. He's supposed to be a bit queer in the head. He was invalided out a few years ago but now he has his own pub not far from here. He'll buy anything you bring. And he'll pay a fair price. Clothing, cutlery, fags, rum, you name it, Ernie'll buy it.' He wiped his mouth with the corner of his handkerchief. 'I met up with him a couple of years ago when I was serving on the Victory - a helluva decent bloke who'd never try to do you. As honest as the day is long is Ernie and not half as barmy as the navy thought he was...'

When the two entered the Jolly Roger pub at the top of Commercial Road, the proprietor, Ernie Richards, warmly greeted George, genuine pleasure lighting up his smile.

'George, me old mate!' He was already pulling him a pint of bitter. 'I heard you was sunk and that only a few survived, but I'm glad you were one of the lucky ones.' George smiled and introduced his oppo, Paddy O'Neill from Ireland. Ernie filled out another pint and pushed the two across the counter.

'Your good health, gentlemen,' he toasted, 'and if you don't come home in 'em, may you always swim away from 'em. And now tell me all about what happened to you.'

Hoskins gave Ernie a quick run down on the events of the fateful night when his ship had been blown apart by the German mine. He didn't mention his own part in saving the officer's life.

The pub was already filling up even though it was only just after 6 o'clock. Ernie listened spellbound, sipping at a glass which O'Neill guessed contained genuine navy rum. When Hoskins finished his story, Ernie filled out two more pints for them. Then he winked covertly at Hoskins. 'Got anything for me?'

George nodded and Ernie pointed to the door leading to the office behind the bar. 'Take your drinks in there, lads, and I'll be with you in a couple of minutes.'

While they waited George took the ten shirts from the gas-mask bags and laid them out neatly on the table.

'How much d'reckon they're worth?' O'Neill whispered to him, his heart beginning to pound. Before Hoskins could answer, the curtains parted and Ernie pushed his way into the office.

'Right then, me old mate, what have we....?' His gaze took in the shirts and he nodded in satisfaction. 'Ah, you're back in the slop room, George.' He grinned. 'You always did manage to get yourself a handy number.' He counted the shirts. 'Size 16, eh? Good, there a ready market for them, what with clothes rationing and so on.' His eyes narrowed to slits as he did some sums in his head. 'Ten at seven and six each. That's three pounds fifteen between you, or one pound seventeen and six a man. Okay?'

Hoskins nodded and O'Neill's breath sagged out of him in a sigh of complete ecstasy. His share represented nearly two weeks pay.

'We have another 190 of them,' Hoskins was saying to Ernie. O'Neill held his breath in disbelief. Ernie nodded, taking the shirts and dropping them in a tea chest in the corner of the office. 'No problem, mate,' he said, 'only don't get caught... and drink up. I'll bring you in another couple of pints and we'll have ourselves a little chat.'

An hour later, they were feeling the warming effect of the drink as they sipped at their fourth pint. O'Neill had his hand in his pocket fingering the notes Ernie had given him and trying at the same time to work out in his head what one hundred and ninety shirts would fetch at seven and six each, divided by two.

'Do me a favour, Ernie,' he heard Hoskins say, 'and show Paddy your...eh...collection.' He elbowed O'Neill in the ribs. 'You'd like to see Ernie's collection, wouldn't you, Paddy?'

O'Neill had no idea what they were talking about but he nodded enthusiastically.

Ernie beamed and downed his rum in one swallow. It was obvious to O'Neill that whatever he collected, Ernie was proud of it. He watched in silence as Ernie unlocked a steel cupboard in the corner of the office and carefully removed a large leather-bound box with brass hinges and a brass lock. He placed it on the table and opened it. O'Neill saw that it was lined in purple velvet and divided into compartments, each containing a sealed jar.

Ernie paused for a few moments for effect and then handed O'Neill a jar with an ornate label on which was printed what appeared to be a Royal Crest and the words 'His Majesty, George V, King and Emperor.'

O'Neill held the jar up to the light, his brow furrowed. He read the label again and looked from Hoskins to Ernie, wondering if they were playing some sort of joke on him. It was quite obvious what the jar contained. They were both looking at him, waiting for him to make comment.

'But - but this is only...' He stopped. Ernie was smiling proudly.

Hoskins nodded. 'Yes,' he prompted, 'only what..?'

O'Neill looked at the object in the jar and then back at Hoskins. 'Only shit...' he said at last.

'Ah yes, Paddy,' Ernie blustered proudly, taking the jar from him and placing it carefully on the table. 'It's shit alright but it's not just any old shit. That's royal shit. That shit was shit by His Majesty, King George the Fifth of England.' He reached into the leather-bound box and handed O'Neill another jar. 'And this one was shit by Her Majesty, Queen Mary, and look, this one was shit by the present king, His Majesty King George the Sixth, and this one by Her Majesty the Queen.' He placed jar after jar in a row on the table. 'And these two here were shit by Princess Elizabeth and Princess Margaret..'

He explained to the bemused O'Neill that he had been an officers' steward on the royal yacht for many years. Obsessed with things royal he had devised a method of trapping the contents of the royal lavatory by inserting a wire net into the outlet pipe which should have emptied into the sea. By establishing who was using the lavatory at any given time, and retrieving the contents of the net immediately after the lavatory was flushed, he had built up his unique collection over a period of years.

'And this is the most prized item of my collection,' Ernie said proudly, handing O'Neill a jar which actually held two faeces.

O'Neill examined the contents trying to contain the feeling of nausea that threatened to make him vomit the four pints he had imbibed too quickly. He looked questioningly at Ernie.

Ernie took the jar and examined it solemnly. 'They were such a lovely pair,' he said, emotion choking his voice. 'That's why I couldn't bear to part 'em, so I put them both in the same jar... so they could be together for ever.'

'Can you still tell which is which, Ernie?' Hoskins belched as he slurped at his pint. Ernie looked at him in surprise, amazed at the stupidity of such a question.

'But of course I can tell 'em apart, me old mate,' he said. 'They're as different as chalk and cheese. The lighter one there, that's Wallis, Mrs. Simpson, later to be the Duchess of Windsor. And the other, that's the Prince of Wales - later to became Edward the Eighth.' He put the jar with the others on the table. 'Unique,' he whispered proudly, 'an absolutely unique collection. There's not a day goes by that I don't take 'em out and fondle and admire 'em - seventeen in all, kings, queens, princes, princesses, ladies in waiting, Lord Louis Mountbatten himself...worth a king's ransom, I'd say, wouldn't you, Paddy me boy?'

O'Neill looked at Hoskins, still not sure if all this was an elaborate joke. Hoskins winked, nodded and finished off his pint. As long as Ernie Richards, officer's steward, invalided from the navy for being a bit barmy in the head, was willing to pay seven and six for Petty Officers' white shirts, O'Neill decided that he too would always be happy to admire the collection of royal shit.

'A truly unique collection, Ernie' he affirmed, hiccuping slightly. 'You are right to be proud of it. Money couldn't buy such a treasure...'

When they left the Jolly Roger, O'Neill looked at his grinning companion. 'You don't believe all that load of old shit, Hoskie, do you?' he asked.

Hoskins laughed. 'You've got a nice way of putting it, Paddy,' he said at last. 'I don't think Ernie is as mad as the navy thinks he is but, anyway, get used to it. You'll be shown that collection every time we visit, and that's going to be fairly often until we get rid of all of you know what..' He pushed his cap to a more jaunty angle. 'Anyway, Paddy, me old mate, let's be off to the Coliseum. Drina is doing the Dance of the Doves there tonight and we don't want to miss out on that...'

The Coliseum, Portsmouth's only strip theatre, stood at the corner of Commercial Road and Queen's Street. It provided the fleet's sailors with a nightly diet of strip-tease, interspersed with blue comedians, magicians, tenors and a leggy chorus line. This all helped to keep naval morale at a noisy height, and also kept the war at sea as far as possible from their sex-starved minds.

Each week, the top billing went to a strip-tease artiste. These shapely ladies constantly vied with each other to think up new more exciting ways of stripping off their clothes while tantalisingly keeping their feminine charms hidden just when the sailors thought all was about to be revealed. This week a lady named Drina was billed to perform the spectacular Dance of the Seven Doves.

'She's good, Paddy,' Hoskins told O'Neill. 'I saw her in Blackpool when I was up there on leave. She comes on dressed in these little veils and she dances around the stage to the music dropping off the veils one by one. And, like, when the veil is just about to drop off, say, her right tit they release a dove up at the back and the timing is just perfect. The veil drops off, you see all her tit for just a second and then the dove arrives, settles on her tit and covers it with its wings. Bloody great! She finishes up bollick naked with a dove on her head, one in each of her hands, two on her tits, one on her navel and the lucky shagger, number seven, sits right there on her quim.'

The Coliseum was packed - the word was around that Drina was good. The front six rows were occupied by what looked like the entire engine room staff of an aircraft carrier lying out in the Solent. This was O'Neill's first visit to the Coliseum and he had never seen so many near-naked women before. He was having bad thoughts already. He wondered what Sister Angela, back in the Convent school in Ireland would think of this sort of carry-on, then dismissed her from his mind.

A Chinese magician was going through his nervous routine on the stage. Like all the minor acts, he was being subjected to good-natured banter and heckling from the noisy audience of sailors. Most of them were well oiled and impatient for Drina to do her stripping act.

Hoskins looked at his watch. 'I'm going for a leak, Paddy,' he whispered. 'I'm bursting. Make sure you hold my seat.'

The Chinese magician was preparing for the grand finale of his act - the Vanishing Lady Trick. His assistant, a scantily clad Oriental lady of uncertain age and buxom proportions, helped him to erect the wardrobe-like box into which he would place her and, hopefully, make her vanish before their eyes. His yellow face was beaded with sweat by the time she was finally locked away. He twisted the ends of his moustache as he leered lecherously down at his noisy audience. Then he tapped the box three times with his wand and slowly opened the door. The box was empty. He turned in triumph to the audience.

'The lady, she is glon,' he cried in feigned amazement, 'she is glon. Vere is she glon?'

Hoskins had returned to his seat. 'Jesus,' he whispered to O'Neill, 'is that fucking Chink still on.?'

'The lady, she is glon,' repeated the Chinese magician, 'vere is she glon?'

Hoskins stood up and cupped his hands around his mouth. 'She flucked off, you stupid clunt,' he shouted, 'and if you'd fluck off with her we could get on with the show.'

A cheer went up from the packed auditorium. The curtain came down quickly and the magician and his reincarnated assistant fled to the wings. Second-rate acts suffered short shrift in Pompey's Coliseum.

'Right,' said Hoskins, 'now we can get on with the big stuff.'

O'Neill sat rigid in his seat. The beautiful Drina, her voluptuous body swaying and writhing to the rhythm of Eastern music played on a flute, was held in the searching spotlight. She paused for a dramatic second, her arms outstretched, her breasts straining through the veils that barely covered them. Her bare belly and shapely thighs jerked with the music. There was a sudden whirring of wings. A white dove flew from the balcony over the heads of the now silent sailors and landed gently on her head. Immediately her body took up the throbbing rhythm and a groan of satisfaction emanated from the spellbound audience.

First the right breast was momentarily bared. O'Neill felt himself stiffen. Then the whirring dove, perfectly timed, arrived to tantalisingly hide its shapely fullness.

'Jesus,' Hoskins groaned, 'I'm afraid I'll blow off right here in my pants.'

The left breast was suddenly bare. Drina swayed sensuously to the music, her arms outstretched. Dove number three spread its protecting wings to hide her curving charms. Immediately three more doves were released. Two flew straight to Drina's outstretched hands while the other perched cheekily on her dimpled navel.

O'Neill's face was red, his eyes glued to Drina's twitching body as she stood centre stage, swaying and jerking in the spotlight. She worked the last veil slowly down, down over her belly and hips. A breathless silence came down on the audience.

Then the veil slipped over Drina's hips and held for a tantalising second before it drifted slowly over her thighs. At long last all was revealed. Vaguely, O'Neill heard the whirring beat of a dove's urgent wings. At the same moment, a voice from the front row shouted 'Now!' and thirty sailors' caps went skimming up into the smoky air. The hapless dove flew straight into the spinning barrage and fell crashing behind the third row.

Drina, blinded by the spotlight, swayed and twisted in her glorious nakedness, waiting for the arrival of the seventh dove. For long seconds she was unaware that her protective cover had been blown by the engine room staff of a fleet carrier.

O'Neill's heart was thumping, his teeth clenched. Drina suddenly realised that she was stark naked standing in front of hundreds of panting sailors. She threw the two doves from her hands in panic and covered herself as best she could as she fled in confusion from the stage of the Coliseum followed by six fluttering doves. O'Neill had seen his first naked woman and he loved it.

The shouts and cheers of the aroused audience followed Drina all the way to her dressing-room. Tonight's performance would go down in naval history as long as tales were told at sea. Every teller would boast that it was his cap that had trapped the dove which should have caressed Drina's naked quim.

'What did I tell you, Paddy?' chortled Hoskins. 'Wasn't that the best show you've ever seen?'

That night, in his bed in Aggie Weston's, O'Neill dreamt that he was dove number seven. He was perched happily on Sister Angela's private parts and she was stroking his head in throbbing ecstasy. He woke up suddenly, his pants a sticky mess. Strangely, after that he never thought of Sister Angela, ever again.

Chapter Four

Liverpool

On June 1st, 1942, the newspaper headlines blazoned that Royal Airforce bombers had dropped over 2,000 tons of bombs on the city of Cologne on the previous night. They had, it was claimed, done more damage in that one raid than in the previous 1,200 raids on the city.

O'Neill, too, had problems. Recently drafted from the barracks in Portsmouth to join His Majesty's aircraft-carrier, Pinewell, presently undergoing refit in Liverpool docks, he peered hopefully into the Green Man's saloon bar in search of Hoskins. Somewhere in its smoky depths he could hear George's unmistakable tenor voice raised in boisterous song:

'.... watching the dockyard kiddies sitting on the dockyard wall, watching their dockyard daddies doing sweet fuck-all...'

A burst of cheers and catcalls went up from the mixed audience when Hoskins finished. O'Neill spotted his mate when he stood up and bowed to acknowledge the boozy applause.

The Green Man pub was located near the gates of Liverpool's King George V Dock. From opening to closing time, each day of every week, sailors, their wives and sweethearts, dockyard workers, ladies of the night - and day - all crowded together in the Green Man's noisy smoke-filled bars. It was here that cash deals for quick knee-tremblers around the corner, or more long-term contracts lasting throughout the night, were quietly struck.

Hoskins was cramped at a table with Supply Chief Petty Officer Hall and Writer Godfrey Wilkins. Writer Wilkins was a good-looking boy of 19 with fair wavy hair, the skin of his face so soft and smooth that it obviously had never felt the dull scrape of a razor. He sipped at a gin and Italian vermouth - he never could stand those awful pints that the Chief drank. On the whole, he found the company he was in rather rough - these Supply chappies particularly could be a trifle crude at times, but he liked Chiefie Hall. At least, he knew how to treat a boy....

Chief Petty Officer Hall hadn't believed it at first when he was notified by the Drafting Office that he was being sent to the aircraft carrier, HMS Pinewall, to take charge of the victualling of the 1,000 or so ratings who formed its crew. His cup of misery overflowed completely when he was ordered to inform Supply Assistant Hoskins, as from that day promoted to Leading Supply Assistant, and Supply Assistant O'Neill that they were to be part of his staff on this new commission.

'This is all your fucking fault,' he groaned at them in the privacy of his office. 'Sure as God, they had me forgotten here till you pair of stupid fucking heroes turned up. You're nothing but bad luck for me...'

O'Neill shifted uncomfortably from one foot to the other. He was thinking about the shirts. They still had sixty to dispose of. If there were going to be a stock-take because the Chief was drafted - Jesus, they'd hang him for sure if he was caught again so soon.

Hoskins was thinking of the shirts too. They had four nights left to get the whole lot ashore and that shouldn't present any great problem. They'd have to raise their productivity levels a peg or two, that was all.

'Not to worry, Paddy,' he reassured O'Neill when they were back up in the loft. 'Even if they do a stock-take, who's to say that we're responsible for anything that might be missing? The crowd down below probably have a few side-liners going too. So just concentrate on the fact that we've got to get the rest of those shirts out of here if we're going to get our money. And stop worrying, will you? There's a bleedin' war on and there's too much going on to keep track of every little bale of stuff that might go missing. Those shirts'll just be written off...'

Hoskins, the new gold anchor signifying the rank of Leading Supply Assistant sparkling on his left sleeve, saw O'Neill across the bar and beckoned him over.

'I thought you were bringing the landlady out for a farewell drink tonight, Paddy.' He gave Chief Petty Officer Hall a knowing nudge. 'Paddy's got a good thing going with his landlady, Chief, though he won't admit it. But I've seen the look on her face in the mornings when she waves him off to work. Wow-ee!' His tongue shot in and out suggestively. 'Her old man's in the Marines but he doesn't come home too often apparently. I reckon she's gasping for it at this stage - she has a sort of a little lost girl look on her face all the time.' He turned to O'Neill for confirmation. 'Isn't that so, Paddy?'

O'Neill's face took on a deeper shade of crimson. 'Ah, shut up, for Chris' sake, Hoskie, will you?' he whispered, 'she's waiting outside -I just wanted to make sure you were here before I brought her in. She's got Pearl with her and, as usual, Pearl wants to go for a feed of fish and chips first.' He paused uncertainly, looking at the Chief and Godfrey. 'Mrs. Perkins doesn't really approve of places like this, especially when she has Pearl with her. She's only a kid, you see... about 16, I'd say...'

Hoskins's interest perked up immediately. Kid or no kid, he thought, if this Pearl bit looked anything like her mother, then he intended to have a go at her before the night was out.

When they joined HMS Pinewell, the crew quarters were still being refitted. The twenty or so ratings forming the advance party were temporarily boarded out in civilian lodgings. O'Neill, through the luck of the draw, was boarded with Mrs. Norma Perkins, wife of Royal Marine Thomas Perkins, currently based at Portsmouth. They had one daughter. Pearl worked in the local munitions factory and was still living at home with her mother. Hoskins, to his utter chagrin and disgust, had been boarded with an elderly couple whose two middle-aged sons lived with them, both dockyard mateys and both confirmed bachelors.

'I'll tell you something for nothing, Chief.' Hoskins sighed. 'When it comes to women, these bloody Irish have all the luck. I'd give a month's bubbly for a go at Paddy's landlady.' He finished his pint in a gulping swallow. 'Tonight, however, I'll settle for the daughter...'

O'Neill scowled at him. 'Look, Hoskie,' he pleaded, 'please don't lay it on with Pearl - she's only a kid. Okay? Mrs. Perkins would shoot the both of us if she thought even for one moment....'

'Forget it, Paddy.' Hoskins grinned. 'I promise I'll be a good boy, I won't lay a finger on her - not unless she grabs hold of me by the you-know-what, that is.' He turned to Chief Hall. 'Just you wait till you see Paddy's bint, Chief,' he told him. 'She's gorgeous and, like I said, she's gasping for it...'

When O'Neill thought about it, which was often since that night in the Coliseum when Drina had awakened his slumbering sexuality, he had to agree that Mrs. Perkins was a beautiful woman but she struck him as being a sad woman too. He couldn't figure out the reason why. Whether she was gasping for it or not, he had noticed that when she bent over him to refill his cup, or perform any of the services that she liked to give her paying guest, she didn't seem to mind when her full, firm breasts brushed against his head.

He felt himself going half hard at the thought of it. But, Jesus, Mrs. Perkins was old enough to be his mother. She might be at least 35, he guessed, and he himself was barely 19. And Pearl was scarcely out of school.

Writer Godfrey Wilkins snuggled up a little closer to Bert Hall. He hated it when these crude supply chappies talked about women in their bawdy sort of way. In fact, he hated it any time that Bert talked about women and he didn't care who noticed it.

'Oh, come on, Bert,' he whispered to the Chief Pusser. 'We don't want to get delayed by these damn women of O'Neill's. You promised that we'd go to the pictures and that we'd go for a - a little walk later on.' His groping hand caressed the Chief's bulging thigh.

'Right, Paddy,' Hoskins said, 'I'll solve all your problems for you. I'll take Pearl for her feed of fish and chips and you wheel her Mammy in here. We'll join you later.'

O'Neill gave him a warning scowl and headed for the door where Norma Perkins and Pearl were still arguing about the chips. Norma, her brown hair tied back with a black ribbon in a rather severe bun, was wearing a tight-fitting white skirt that hugged her slim hips, and a floral silk blouse that wobbled with every movement of her body. Pearl, small and blonde, with a doll-like face, wore a navy blue jacket and a tight grey skirt, which ended inches above her shapely knees and tantalisingly showed the imprint of the suspenders, which held up her silk stockings.

Hoskins' quick intake of breath showed how impressed he was - but it was at Pearl he was looking. O'Neill introduced him and had to give him a nudge before he released Pearl's hand.

'Right,' said Hoskins to Norma, 'I understand your lovely daughter here is feeling peckish and so am I - a feed of fish and chips would fill the bill nicely.' He gave Norma his most disarming smile when he saw the unease on her face. 'Not to worry, Mrs. Perkins,' he charmed, 'I'll have her back to you safe as houses as soon as we've eaten...' He turned his smile on Pearl. 'Promise your mother you won't do anything she wouldn't do...?'

Pearl giggled and threw a farewell smile over her shoulder, glad to escape from her mother's custody. 'Don't worry, Mammy.' She smiled. 'I can handle this fellow, no bother.' She linked arms with Hoskins and they headed for the fish and chip shop around the corner.

Norma hesitated, looking after them. 'He seems a nice boy,' she said. 'Is he?'

O'Neill nodded vigorously. 'Don't worry, Mrs. Perkins. Hoskie is all noise and no bite. Pearl'll have him eating out of her hand....' At least, I hope she will, he thought.

O'Neill introduced the Chief and Godfrey to Norma, glad that the overexuberant Hoskie was out of the way while Norma settled down.

'Pleased to meet you, Chief,' Norma said to Bert Hall. Though she was smiling, O'Neill immediately detected a note of disapproval in her voice. 'I see you're a regular navy man,' she said to the Chief, 'not like these young chaps here, just in for the war...' Her hazel eyes turned a smile on O'Neill. Bert Hall decided that Hoskins was right - old enough to be his mother, this bint might be but she was obviously carrying a torch for O'Neill. A blind man could see that. 'My husband, Thomas, is in the Marines, based in Portsmouth...'

The Chief hauled himself to his feet and took Norma's hand in his. 'Pleased to meet you, maam,' He was smiling lasciviously. 'I hear you're looking after O'Neill here very well...' His voice trailed off suggestively and O'Neill squirmed inside himself. Norma's eyes swivelled to Writer Wilkins who had remained seated, his hand back on Bert's knee. O'Neill was surprised at the puzzled look that puckered her face. Then she smiled thinly, her eyebrows raised in an arched question.

'A writer? I don't believe I ever met a Navy writer before. And come to think about it, I never met anybody named Godfrey before either. What a....a nice name! How d'you do?'

She didn't hold out her hand. Wilkins's eyes met hers in a challenging stare. Then he emptied his drink in one gulp and coughed when it caught in his breath. He realised that Norma had sensed the relationship that existed between himself and Bert, and that she disapproved of brown hatters. Not that I care a damn what you think, you stupid bitch, he thought.

'I'm very well, Mrs. Perkins.' He smiled archly. Godfrey had decided to show this cow that he could be as bitchy as the next when it came down to the cutting barbs that usually hurled through the jealous air when members of the fair sex met up with the likes of him.

'Did you say your husband's name was Thomas,' he asked. 'Tom Perkins! A big, tall, ever so good-looking marine?' Norma nodded dumbly, suddenly apprehensive. 'You know something, dearie, I believe I met up with him one night in Portsmouth. We went dancing together at the South Parade Pier. Such a....a big man! You're so lucky...'

Bert Hall laughed nervously and swallowed his drink. Satisfied that he had easily won that encounter, Godfrey pulled Bert to his feet and they left the Green Man together. Godfrey's hand surreptitiously held on to Bert's elbow. Norma Perkins slumped into the vacated seat, a flush of anger reaching up from her neck to suffuse her cheeks. O'Neill felt that there was something amiss but he couldn't quite put his finger on it.

'Do you - how could you possibly associate with - that sort of person, Jimmy?' Norma's question was bubbling with indignation. 'I mean - how long have you known him? Don't you realise what he is, the awful type of person he is...'

O'Neill saw the tears glistening in her eyes. He was still at a loss. He knew perfectly well that there was something different about Godfrey, something girlish, and he'd heard him being dismissed as a brown hatter, but he had never been able to pluck up the courage to ask what a brown hatter was.

O'Neill was now totally at a loss. His every instinct wanted to reach out to Norma, to take her hand in his and comfort her, but, Jesus, he couldn't do a thing like that, for God's sake? I mean... He went up to the bar and got a gin and tonic for Norma and a pint for himself.

'Look, Mrs. Perkins...' he started when he put the drinks on the table and squeezed in beside her. Norma took his hand in hers, a smile twisting her lips. He wanted so badly to kiss her.

'Norma,' she said, looking into his eyes. 'Call me Norma, Jimmy, for God's sake. I may be your landlady, and even that finishes tomorrow morning, but you don't have to be so formal all the time, love, do you?' She took O'Neill's hand and held it discreetly under the table.

He felt his insides melt with the joy of it. 'I'm sorry about Godfrey, I mean.' His confusion made him stutter. 'I don't really know him at all. It's the Chief.... What did he say to upset you? I mean....'

Norma sighed and sipped at her drink. She took one of O'Neill's cigarettes from the packet on the table and he lit it for her. 'It - it's my husband,' she said at last. 'It's about, Tom, my husband.' She sighed again. 'It's all so humiliating, Jimmy, I don't even know if I should tell you....'

A neighbour, a good friend of hers, had first hinted it to her. The friend's husband had joined the Marines at the same time as Tom and, as she had got it from him, Tom Perkins seemed to be spending all his time with brown hatters down Queen Street in Portsmouth.

'Oh, I get my allowance every week, as usual,' Norma told O'Neill, 'but my husband hasn't been my husband for over a year now. He never comes home on leave, he never writes....' She stubbed out the half-smoked cigarette. 'It's all so humiliating, Jimmy. Jesus, I hate him when I think about what he's done to me.' She sniffed. O'Neill wanted to take her in his arms. 'We used to be so happy, you know, before this damn war started. He was manager down at Duffy's butchers shop and he was making good money, and now?' She shrugged. 'He prefers things like that Godfrey person to me, his wife...' She sipped at her drink.

O'Neill took a long swallow at his pint, unsure what to say. Hoskins and Pearl arrived back in the pub. Norma blew her nose to hide the tears glimmering in her eyes. O'Neill sighed with relief and stood up.

'Can I get you two a drink?' he asked. Pearl looked at Hoskins and he shook his head.

'No, thanks, Paddy,' he said. 'Pearl and I are going dancing. We just came in to tell you. There's a do down at the Toc-H....' He was watching Norma's face. What's Paddy been at, he thought, she's been crying. Pearl nodded her agreement and cut off the protest that she saw forming in her mother's eyes.

'I'll be alright, Mammy,' she insisted. She grinned at Hoskins. 'He's only a big baby, really.' Before Norma could offer any more protest or warning, Pearl and Hoskins waved and left the bar.

O'Neill turned to her mother. 'Pearl'll be alright, Mrs...Norma,' he reassured her, his hand touching hers and holding it. He felt more confident now that Hoskins and Pearl were out of the way. Norma squeezed his hand. She moved a little closer to him.

'What d'say, Norma?' O'Neill asked, 'why don't we have one more drink here and then you and I'll go dancing too.' He saw the doubt in her eyes. 'Not to the Toc-H, of course,' She smiled at him, quick excitement flooding her. 'Why don't we take a train into town. They usually have a fairly good do at the YMCA...'

The YMCA was practically empty. 'Good God,' said O'Neill, 'the last time I was here you couldn't move.' They paused uncertainly. Then he saw the piano in the corner. He took Norma's hand and led her across the room. 'I'll do a bit of serenading while we wait for this place to wake up,' he told her.

He sat down and ran his fingers over the keys. It wasn't a Steinway but it was in tune. Norma sat beside him.

'I didn't know you could play the piano, Jimmy,' she said. 'There's so much I don't know about you.'

'What's your favourite tune, Norma?' he asked.

She thought for a moment. 'Maria Elena. Do you know it?'

He nodded and started playing. Norma listened rapturously. O'Neill smiled and started singing softly to her. '....Maria Elena, you're the answer to a prayer. Maria Elena, can't you see how much I care...'

Norma stood behind him, her hands resting on his shoulders. She swayed in rhythm with him, their bodies touching. 'To me your voice is like the echo of a sigh, And when you're near, my heart can't speak above a sigh...'

Just then, the air-raid sirens wailed. Norma jumped in fright, her face going pale. O'Neill stood up from the piano and took her hand protectively as they hurried out of the building. All around them people were rushing to the shelters, fear showing on some faces, bravado on others, most, however, wearing a mask of calm and numbed acceptance. The people of Liverpool were getting used to Jerry's nocturnal visits.

O'Neill took Norma's arm and squeezed it. He wasn't sure what he should do. After all, he was a member of His Majesty's Navy, supposed to be out there fighting the enemy face to face, rather than cowering in shelters, which were for civilians.

'Do you want to go to the shelter, or what, Norma?' he asked, glancing up at the darkening sky. The distant sound of anti-aircraft fire began to rumble, gun-flashes lighting and darkening the clouds. It had started to drizzle.

Norma pulled her coat tighter about her. 'The shelter, Jimmy, please,' she said anxiously. 'I - I don't like this sort of thing....' She felt his arm going around her shoulder and she huddled against him.

The shelter was packed but they managed to find room on a bench. Norma was obviously terrified and O'Neill pulled her close to him, her head buried in his chest, his arms tightly about her.

'Down, everybody,' shouted the warden from the door. Everybody bent forward in their seats trying desperately to protect themselves from whatever danger was about to envelop them. Norma's quick intake of breath betrayed her terror.

'Not to worry, sweetheart,' O'Neill whispered, feeling delicious pleasure when his lips touched her ear. 'We'll be okay.'

A sudden blast breeze swept through the shelter and they heard a violent explosion not far away. Norma clung to O'Neill. He could feel her heart pounding and he squeezed her to him comfortingly.

'Okay, everybody,' the warden called, a few minutes later. 'It was a land-mine and it landed a few streets away. I saw it parachuting down...'

Half an hour later the all-clear wailed and a hum of conversation buzzed once again through the crowded shelter. Norma lifted her face and smiled her relief. O'Neill could feel her breath on his cheek. He hesitated for a moment. Then his lips touched on hers, gently at first, then more firmly, then almost fiercely as he felt the urgent passion burning between them. After what seemed an eternity of wonder, Norma pushed him gently from her, her cheeks burning.

'Oh, Jimmy, Jimmy,' she whispered. 'We shouldn't - we mustn't....'

O'Neill smiled down at her and pulled her to him. 'Why mustn't we?' he demanded, new-found confidence flooding through him. He kissed her again. She resisted and then let herself go.

'Okay, okay, the show's over, ladies and gentlemen, please...' The warden's voice boomed through the shelter. Norma pushed herself out of O'Neill's embrace and flopped back on the bench.

'Behave yourself, sailor,' she whispered, embarrassed to find that they were alone in the shelter. 'That's more than enough - for now.' O'Neill noted the promise in her voice and the sparkle in her eye.

'Okay, sweetheart,' he smiled, his arm encircling her waist. 'Let's get ourselves another drink and then we'll go dancing. I feel in form for it after that....'

Norma looked at her watch. 'I have a better idea, Jimmy,' she suggested. 'We'll have another drink and we'll go home - you have to be up early in the morning...'

O'Neill grimaced. Jesus, just when he was getting things going he'd have to live back on the ship. Still, it would be a week or ten days before they sailed and he'd be able to see Norma every night. He was looking forward to that.

It was 10.30 when they arrived home. Norma checked to see if Pearl was in her room. Some hope, O'Neill thought, not with Hoskie on the job!

'I wonder where they can be,' Norma asked anxiously when she came back into the front room. O'Neill let his gaze drift up and down her body, excitement filling him. He reached out and took her in his arms. He kissed her. She giggled and then responded. His hand slipped down and closed over her firm breast. She let him fondle it for a moment and then pulled his hand away, at the same time pressing her thighs firmly against his. He could feel himself hardening and from the way she was wriggling against him, he knew that she could feel it too. Just then, they heard the key turning in the front door lock. Shag it anyway, O'Neill thought as Norma pulled away from him. She gave him a quick peck on the lips and went into the kitchen to put on the kettle.

'Oh, there you are, dear,' she called to Pearl, 'I was getting worried about you, what with the air-raid and everything. Is George gone....? Will you have a cup of tea?'

Hoskins had seen O'Neill wiping lipstick off his mouth. Oh-oh, he thought, Paddy's been at it.

'Not for me, Mrs. Perkins,' he said, grabbing Pearl and giving her a quick kiss. O'Neill shook his head warningly. 'I have to be off or I'll be locked out. My landlady's very strict...' He stuck his tongue out at O'Neill.

Norma came out of the kitchen and looked at Pearl. She seemed satisfied that nothing untoward had happened. Pearl followed Hoskins to the front door and O'Neill avoided Norma's eyes when he heard Pearl's stifled giggles. Hoskins was at it again.

'Off to bed with you, Jimmy,' Norma whispered. 'You never have tea and I want a quiet chat with Pearl. And we all have to be up early in the morning....'

He gave her a quick kiss. 'Good-night, Pearl,' he called. 'I'll see you tomorrow.' He went up to his room, vaguely disappointed but at the same time, delighted at the way things had turned out. He drew back the blackout curtains before he got into bed. A large moon lit up the room and he hoped that Jerry wouldn't be back again. He was still awake when he heard Norma and Pearl going to their rooms. He sighed happily. It had been a helluva day... one helluva day... He was soon asleep, his dreams filled with urgent desires.

He woke suddenly to find moonlight still flooding the room. He felt a warm body cuddling up against him, a groping hand moving up and down his back. He sat up in surprise. The hand closed over his mouth cutting off his startled gasp.

'Ssh, Jimmy,' he heard Norma's whisper. 'For God's sake don't make any noise. You'll wake Pearl....'

Jimmy flopped back in the bed, the blood beginning to race uncontrollably through him. He felt his penis hardening when his arms reached around Norma's body and he felt the silk night-gown clinging to her. Their mouths met in a hard kiss. She slid her arms around his neck and pressed against him.

'Oh, Jimmy, Jimmy darling,' she whispered, 'This is a wrong thing for me to do but I couldn't let you go without - without getting to know you properly.' She lifted her head and looked at him. He could barely make out the anxious face framed in the halo of brown hair released from the bun she usually wore..

'You could never do anything wrong, sweetheart,' he whispered between kisses. Tentatively, he pulled at her nightdress till it was up to her waist, and he slipped his hand inside to cup her full breast, moving from one to the other. His penis slipped between her thighs as she pressed to him. She gave a sighing groan when his hand moved down hesitatingly to caress the little mound of hair between her legs. His heart pounded when his searching fingers touched into her. He paused, no longer sure of himself. Was he supposed to do it now or what? Norma jerked as she came.

'Please, Jimmy darling,' she pleaded. 'Please....' She lifted her head and looked at him. Then she guessed. 'Is - is it your first time?' she whispered, a rush of maternal love flooding her.

O'Neill nodded dumbly, suddenly ashamed. Norma rolled onto her back and pulled him gently on top of her. She slipped her hand down between them and gripped his throbbing penis. 'My, what a big boy you are. Jimmy,' she whispered, caressing him gently. Jimmy suppressed a groan, afraid he was going to come before he started. Norma guided his penis into her. She groaned aloud as she came again. Then her legs stiffened straight, matching his frenzied rhythmic motion. His two hands were up under her nightdress, each one full with a breast, thumbs and forefingers gently pulling at the nipples. Her arms were tight about his neck, her lips burnt to his. The rhythm quickened uncontrollably. Suddenly he felt his insides emptying into her and he thought he'd die with the joy of it.

'Norma, Norma,' he whispered breathlessly, wriggling against her.

'Oh, Jimmy darling,' she whispered back. 'That was the most wonderful thing that ever happened to me.' She pushed up hard against him and groaned.

They rolled over carefully to lie on their sides, his wilting penis firmly held inside her. They lay there exhausted, one of his hands on her breast, the other rubbing on the full cheek of her bottom. Then Norma's hand slid down and touched under him, caressing him gently. He groaned in ecstasy as his penis seemed to leap up and fill out inside her. Norma sighed. She rolled over on top of him, her legs open, his spreading penis trapped inside her. Slowly, rhythmically she controlled the pace of their love.

'Oh my God,' she groaned helplessly, 'it just keeps happening. I keep coming all the time...'

O'Neill was happy just to lie there for ever. Gently they explored one another's naked bodies, kissing and caressing, feeling and cuddling till at last Jimmy fell into deep exhausted sleep. For minutes Norma listened to his steady breathing, her head on his bare chest. Then reluctantly she drew back the covers and slid out of bed. In the light of the moon still streaming though the window she could see his boyish face, his hair tousled, his lips apart in a smile.

'Goodbye, darling,' she whispered. 'I love you and I always will...' Gently she kissed him and tip-toed back to her room.

When O'Neill woke he felt the warm body still pressing against him, her hand gently caressing his penis which was hard and unyielding. The joy of the earlier night surged through him. He sighed and slipped one arm around her neck, the other hand closing over her naked breast. He caressed its fullness and wriggled down to touch the nipple gently with his lips. He heard her groaning pleasure when his hand slipped down between her legs to explore and touch inside her. She was holding his penis in her hand. She squeezed it gently.

'God, Paddy, that's a whopper you've got there!' O'Neill stopped, hardly able to believe his ears. He looked down in disbelief at the cheeky face smiling up at him in the pale light of the dawn chinking through the window.

'Jesus,' he said aloud. 'Pearl!' Her hand tightened on his penis in warning. 'What are you doing here?'

She grinned up at him.. 'Hush, Paddy for God's sake!' Her hand closed over his mouth. 'Who did you think it was for feck's sake- my mother?'

'O'Neill collapsed back on the pillow, his penis deflating in his shocked surprise. Pearl massaged it urgently.

'Come on, Paddy,' she whispered at him, 'don't back off now.' She pulled him on top of her, her legs opening in invitation.

'Fuck me, Paddy,' she pleaded, 'fuck me, please, before my insides melt away...'

O'Neill felt reluctant desire well up inside him. His penis stiffened in her hand. She guided it into herself and picked up the flowing rhythm of his movement, her arms pulling him tight against her.

'Oh, Paddy, Paddy,' she whispered, 'you're filling every nook and cranny inside me.' She groaned in ecstasy. They came together in a shuddering torrent of pleasure. He could only manage it once more despite Pearl's efforts to keep him erect.

The opening light of dawn was creeping around the room when she reluctantly slipped out of the bed. She stood beside it and lifted her long blonde hair high above her head. O'Neill watched her as, naked and totally unashamed, she flaunted her small shapely body before him. Her breasts were rounded and small, the pink nipples standing erect. The small shock of blonde curly hair between her shapely thighs protruded provocatively. One hand dropped, caressing it. Her eyes laughed, mocking O'Neill.

Unable to take any more, he threw back the bedclothes and they stood naked facing one another. Her gaze explored his body slowly. Then her arms went around his neck, and she pressed to him, coaxing him, teasing him.

When she felt he was ready, she flopped back onto the bed, her legs wide, pulling him down on top of her. She slid his penis in and locked her legs around his waist, holding him, pressing him deeper and deeper.

'I knew I could make you fuck me again, Paddy,' she whispered breathlessly. 'Oh Jesus, I'm coming....' She sighed happily. 'God help me, Paddy but you sure are some operator...'

Chapter Five

The Irish Sea

'Good morning, staff!'

'Good morning, sir!'

O'Neill stifled a yawn when Supply Warrant Officer Smyth offered the staff of the Victualling Office the traditional morning greeting which heralded the dawning of one more boring day. His thoughts strayed back nostalgically to the converted cupboard that had been his office on the Manway. Small it might have been but it was spacious compared with this present set-up, and it had been his own.

The eight-strong victualling staff on the Pinewell, one officer and seven ratings, were cramped back to back, elbow to elbow, six of them at a long desk facing one blank bulkhead and the other two at a desk facing the opposite, and equally blank, bulkhead. To add to the discomfort, there was no porthole in the compartment, the office being one deck below water level, Above their heads, the fans and generators pumping air into the compartment produced an on-going mixture of hum and buzz that was deafening.

Supply Warrant Officer Smyth had a bad hangover and he had seen O'Neill's gaping yawn.

'Christ, Chief,' he intoned loudly. 'I've seen piss-holes in the snow before this but those eyes of O'Neill's - how the hell did he get them back that far in his head? You'd better see to it that he wears boxing gloves in his hammock or he'll pull himself apart.'

An obliging chuckle from the staff followed his sally. Satisfied that he had set the right tone for the day ahead, Smyth took his seat at the desk just inside the sliding door, beside the bulkhead telephone.

It was 09.00 hours on June 2nd, the supply staff's first day fully victualled on HMS Pinewell. The remainder of the ship's company, including a detachment of Royal Marines, had arrived on board at 07.00 hours.

O'Neill's face reddened and he kept his head down, giving all his attention to the list he was preparing of supplies to be drawn this morning from the ship's refrigerator. Stupid bollicks, he whispered. Hoskins gave him a sympathetic kick under the desk to warn him to keep his cool. O'Neill knew there was going to be more - lots more.

'I understand that O'Neill's a bit of a lad with the women, sir,' Chief Hall responded obligingly to the Warrant Officer's remark. 'These last few weeks when he's been living ashore, I gather he was on the job most of the time. Lucky it didn't fall off, if you ask me. Maybe you should order him to see the medical officer...'

The Chief still believed that he'd have got through the war in the safety of his slop room in Portsmouth if he hadn't been saddled with two heroes like O'Neill and Hoskins. Their volunteering to get back to sea as soon as possible had definitely drawn the Drafting Officer's attention to himself.

'And his mate Hoskins is just as bad,' he added. 'Never manages to get his mind any higher than his bollicks, he doesn't. We've got ourselves a couple of sex maniacs there, I'm afraid, sir.' The Chief was enjoying the suppressed sniggers of the staff and decided to go for broke. 'My, God, I wouldn't feel safe if I was alone with either of 'em here in the office...'

O'Neill's head went down lower but Hoskins resented the fact that his name was now being drawn into a discussion which had started out to examine the topic of O'Neill's hammock habits.

'If I was alone here in the office with you, Chief,' he rejoined cheekily, 'I know whose arse would be in danger, and it wouldn't be yours...'

There was a knock on the door and it slid open. A tall, muscular marine came into the office, his pencil-thin moustache bristling over a row of white teeth. His gaze took in the occupants of the office and stopped at Warrant Officer Smyth. The marine came to attention. 'Marine Perkins reporting for duty, sir,' he barked. 'I have been detailed by the Sar'ant Major to take over the ship's butcher's duties.'

O'Neill thought he was going to be sick. The pen slipped from Hoskins's fingers and made a blob on the large page of the 'Bible' - the inventory of all provisions stored on H.M.S. Pinewell. He dabbed at the spreading ink with a piece of blotting-paper and kept his head down. The last person he wanted to meet right now was Pearl's daddy, especially after the things she'd said about him last night. Chief Petty Officer Hall's brow furrowed as the name jogged at his memory and then he too remembered where he'd heard it before. So this was the handsome brute who was Godfrey's marine boyfriend in Pompey!

This is it, thought O'Neill. This is where I get taken to the slaughter-house to be butchered. He saw the Chief gathering himself together to clear the decks. He's going to enjoy this...

'Right, Perkins,' said Chief Hall, 'O'Neill here is the Assistant in charge of the refrigerator. He will supervise the withdrawal of all provisions every morning at 09.30 hours. You report down here to him. You will also be responsible for dishing out the rum issue.' He paused and then added: 'And I want it known from the beginning that if there is any attempt at fiddling with the ship's company's provisions, I will come down on you like a ton of bricks. Is that understood?'

Warrant Officer Smyth looked sideways at his Chief, puzzled that he should be so openly hostile to the new butcher. Hall avoided the questioning glance, jealousy welling up inside him.

After they left the Green Man last night, Godfrey had gone on about Big Tom Perkins and how handsome he was, delighting that Chiefie Hall was obviously burning with jealousy. They'd finished up having quite a tiff over it but that only made the making up so much sweeter. And now Godfrey's lover was on board the Pinewell. By Christ, thought Bert Hall, no stupid leatherneck is going to fuck up my love life by trying to get off with Godfrey again. No bloody way.

'You have the withdrawals list ready, O'Neill?' The Chief's head swivelled to where O'Neill was trying to hide. O'Neill nodded dumbly. 'Right, off you go then and make sure there's no fiddling. Weigh every pound of meat that comes out of the Cold Room and see that it's accounted for properly or you'll end up in the glass-house with him...' O'Neill grabbed his clip-board and hustled Perkins out of the office, glad to escape.

'Good Christ, what's wrong with the Pusser?' Tom Perkins demanded as they made their way through the stokers' mess-deck to the refrigerator, two decks below. 'Is he always like a cat with a sore arse or what?'

O'Neill's stomach was sick. He was so worn out from the activities of the previous night that he could hardly think. But think he must, and think fast too! Then, like a flash from Heaven, he saw a way out.

'I -I think it might be - be Godfrey!' he stammered at last. Yeah, yeah, that's good thinking. It was all becoming obvious to O'Neill now. Chiefie Hall was dead jealous of Perkins, that was it! O'Neill had noticed the scowl he gave Godfrey in the pub when he started talking about Tom Perkins and how well they got on together in Pompey, how good a dancer he was, how big he was and so on.

Watching the handsome face, the lithe body, the tanned arms stretching with hard muscle as Perkins strained at the heavy hatches, O'Neill almost felt sorry for the poor Chief with his bulging belly and his scrawny body and his horn-rimmed specs. He wouldn't have a chance if it came to a straight contest for Godfrey's heart - or whatever part of him he was interested in. No wonder he was burning with jealousy.

'Godfrey, for Christ's sake?' Tom Perkins demanded. 'Who the fuck is Godfrey?' They were at the door of the refrigerator's air lock and were donning their duffle coats. O'Neill sighed. Things were beginning to take shape in his mind. He was glad now that he'd gotten the chance to talk to Tom Perkins before the Chief or Godfrey twisted the facts about Norma and himself to their warped way of thinking. He put a cigarette in his mouth and offered the packet to Perkins.

'Relax for a minute, Butch,' he said, squatting down on the step of the ladder leading down from the mess-decks, 'and I'll bring you up to date on what's been happening aboard this tub over the last few weeks.' He filled his lungs with welcome smoke and exhaled. 'It's a long story....' And you'd better tell it good, he told himself.

Tom Perkins heard him out in silence, his face reddening or scowling as the facts unfolded. Only once did he interrupt O'Neill and that was when he told how he had innocently brought Mrs. Perkins and Pearl to the Green Man for a farewell drink. They had, unfortunately, met up with the Chief and Godfrey, and Godfrey had told her 'that you and he were - were friends and that you used to take him dancing in Pompey...'

'Jesus! He told her that? The stupid loudmouthed bastard! That was over a year ago...' Perkins stubbed out his cigarette on the step of the ladder, avoiding O'Neill's eyes. 'Did - did Norma know.. I mean... did she know what he - what he was talking about?'

O'Neill, gaining confidence, played his cards masterfully. 'Norma? Oh, you mean Mrs. Perkins. I - I didn't know your wife's name was Norma.' Then he nodded, stubbing out his own cigarette. 'Yes. I think she did. Yes, she did...'

A sudden thought hit Perkins. 'Little Pearl! Does Pearl know too? Did she hear that loudmouth saying - saying whatever it was he said....?' He appeared to be genuinely worried.

O'Neill thought about it and then shook his head. 'I don't know if Pearl knows or not. She wasn't there at the time. She'd gone for fish and chips with Hoskie...'

Perkins sighed in relief. 'Thank God for that, at least,' he said slowly. 'Little Pearl is so - so innocent, you know, like. I'd hate her to know anything like that. She's only a little girl...' O'Neill nodded and said nothing.

Perkins sighed again. 'Jesus, just because a fellow prefers to have his bit of meat filleted....'

O'Neill looked at him, puzzled. 'Filleted...?'

'Yeah, filleted - no bloody bone in the way.' He looked sideways at O'Neill. 'A feed of arse, for Chris' sake, and these bloody women go on and on...' His voice trailed off.

O'Neill stood up. 'We'd better get the stuff up to the galley or we'll have the Chief Cook after us as well as the Pusser..' He decided that he'd handled everything excellently so far.

Just then the Chief Petty Officer Steward in charge of the Wardroom catering arrived with his helper trailing behind him. He nodded to O'Neill and waited till the butcher went into the Cold Room.

'You in charge of this end, Jack?' he asked O'Neill. O'Neill nodded. The Steward lowered his voice to a whisper. 'I take it we'll be able to come to an - an arrangement about prices and things, yes?'

O'Neill nodded again. He was well accustomed now to handling this sort of deal.

'Good,' said the Chief Steward. Then: 'Will you be cutting in the butcher?'

O'Neill thought about it. 'Yes, Chief,' he whispered back. 'I think 'twould be safer to cut him in - just in case. But give it a few days. I've only just got to meet him and I'm not too sure what he's like....'

The Chief Steward nodded his agreement. 'Good thinking, Jack,' he said. 'I'll be in touch and we'll work things out as we go along...'

O'Neill nodded and went in to supervise the withdrawal of the day's supplies. Everything was more or less back to normal. At least, he fervently hoped so...

✣ ✣ ✣ ✣ ✣

Norma Perkins cried as she lay awake in bed waiting for Pearl to come home from her date with George Hoskins. He seemed such a nice boy and Norma hoped that, perhaps, something would come out of it for Pearl. HMS Pinewell was leaving Liverpool tomorrow morning at 07.00 hours, bound for God's knows where.

She thought of Jimmy O'Neill and a delicious thrill shivered through her body. Hoskins had brought her a lovely letter from O'Neill. In it he said he loved her and that he would always love her. She cried when he quoted from Maria Elena and said that it would always be their song. He said he was sorry he couldn't call around himself, but he knew she'd understand. She did understand and she wondered if she'd ever see him again.

Her husband, Tom, had called earlier in the evening, just after Pearl had gone out with George. Norma had told him she never wanted to see him again and slammed the door in his face. She sighed and started crying again. This damn war was tearing her life apart.

CHAPTER SIX

THE NORTHERN APPROACHES

09.00 hours, June 8th. 1942. HMS Pinewell took nearly an hour to work her tortuous way out of the Queen's Dock, and into the muddy water of the River Mersey. Three fussy tugs pulled at their bulky charge, coaxing her into position despite the gusting winds and swirling currents that swept through the Bay of Liverpool.

High on the island overlooking the flight-deck, Captain Hastings, R.N. looked back at the sprawling city, the smoke from the fires of last night's bombing raid still lifting to the sky. He was glad to be leaving it behind. A dedicated officer of the old school, he had been desk-bound for four years at the Admiralty. At an age when he feared that he'd never feel the buck of a deck to his feet again, and the lick of the salt on his face he was given command of the Pinewell.

He went out on to the bridge wing and looked down with fond pride at Pinewell's flowing lines as she swayed and lifted gently in the rising sea. Once a battleship, she had been transformed into an aircraft carrier, with a complement of 852 officers and ratings, including the aircrews of the squadrons of Swordfish and Seafires which were due to fly on later in the evening.

All in all, Captain Hastings reassured himself proudly, the old lady and himself should be able to look after themselves in any situation that might arise. Even up there on the high bridge he could feel the comforting throb of her powerful engines waiting impatiently for the ring of the engine room telegraph that would cast off the tugs' restraining hawsers. Then she would plunge northwards into the Irish Sea and on into the cold, heaving restless waters of the North Atlantic.

Only he knew, at this stage, that Pinewell's mission was to rendezvous off Northern Ireland with a convoy now steaming out of Glasgow and heading for the United States. Pinewell was to provide air-cover till the convoy was well clear of the killing grounds of the North Atlantic. Then she would veer on course to Bermuda where they would carry out two weeks of trials and training for the new flight crews. He would inform the ship's company later on in the evening when Pinewell was well away from listening ears and prying eyes. Thoughts of Bermuda, he felt, should cheer them up.

Below in the Victualling Office, O'Neill looked forward to 'Up Spirits', hoping that a shot of rum would lift his flagging mood. He was working on the Wardroom Repayment Book and no matter how he checked and cross-checked the figures they just wouldn't balance. He hadn't managed to visit Norma before they left Liverpool but his thoughts were constantly of her. He wrote her a letter which Hoskins delivered. In it he had quoted: 'Maria Elena, say that we will never part. Maria Elena, take me to your heart...' Maria Elena will always be our song, he told her. I will always love you.

'You awake, O'Neill?' The Chief's sarcastic question brought him back to the present. 'Take this draft menu down to the Paymaster Commander's cabin for his approval. Then type it and take it back to him for his signature. After that get it stencilled and put a copy on each of the notice-boards on the mess-decks. And give a copy to the Chief Cook. He likes to know what he's supposed to be cooking. Think you can manage that without making too much of a fuck-up of it?'

O'Neill squeezed his way out of the office, glad of the opportunity to get a breath of fresh air and one last look at Liverpool. He stood on the starboard well-deck and watched the tugs pushing as they made their way out into the Bay. Then he climbed the ladder to the deck above where Butch Perkins and his assistant, Marine Davies had their butchers' shop. Perkins was carving a side of beef. Davies was smoking a cigarette which he had rolled from pipe tobacco. O'Neill's nose wrinkled when he got the whiff.

'Don't fucking say it,' growled Davies. 'I like the taste and the smell, even if no-one else does.'

O'Neill's eyebrows lifted. 'My, my, aren't we all very touchy today,' he said, 'and I wasn't going to say anything. I just want a quiet word with Butch here about the amount of mutton issued to the Wardroom Steward yesterday.'

He winked at Butch and beckoned him out to the passageway.

The tugs' sirens hooted in farewell salute as the hawsers were cast off and they felt the surging strength when Pinewell's propellers bit purposefully into the dark grey waters of the Irish Sea. O'Neill and Perkins stood at the rail in silence looking back towards Liverpool, now fading in the distance. They were both wondering when, if ever, they'd be back there again.

'How - how is Mrs. Perkins?' O'Neill asked hesitantly. 'She okay? I was sorry I couldn't get to see her and thank her for - for the way she looked after me.'

Perkins lips tightened. 'I went to see her last night – for all the good it did me. She slammed the door in my face and told me she didn't want to see me again.' He pulled on his cigarette. 'Hard to blame her, I suppose, after what fucking loudmouth told her..'

A last hoot from the tugs and Pinewell's answering siren drowned out the shrieks of the hundreds of sea-gulls diving and fighting to feast on the harvest thrown up in her spumy wake. 'Something wrong with the Wardroom mutton?' Butch's question was tinged defensively. He wasn't sure yet where he stood with O'Neill. All these bloody Supply people stuck together and he hadn't forgotten the Chief Pusser's open hostility to him on the day he arrived

O'Neill glanced back to the butcher's caboose. Davies was attacking the side of beef with a cleaver, his thick arms bulging with muscle. He wasn't paying any attention to them. Butch looked at the Wardroom Repayment Chit that O'Neill handed him and nodded.

'Mutton, 48 lbs,' he read. 'That's what they got and that's what the Chief Steward signed for. Look, there's his moniker. What's the problem?'

O'Neill shook his head. He felt nervous as he always did when he was about to close a deal. What if Butch wouldn't co-operate? What if he reported him to the Chief Pusser?

'No problem, Butch.' He lowered his voice, looked around again and showed the butcher the draft General Mess menu prepared by the Chief for the following week. His finger indicated that next Friday's dinner was going to be roast mutton with mint sauce, carrots, roast and boiled potatoes, followed by spotted Dick and custard.

'That'll be about 300 lbs of mutton we'll have to give down to the Chief Cook in the General Mess galley. Okay?' Butch nodded. 'Now, if I were to charge the Wardroom for 28 lbs of mutton instead of 48 lbs, and you were to make up the difference by leaving the Chief Cook 20 lbs short....'

It was the butcher's turn to look warily around. His mate was still hacking at the side of beef. Pinewell had gathered speed and was heading north. The misty outline of the Isle of Man loomed on her starboard bow.

'What's in it for me, Jack?' Perkins's voice was guarded. 'Apart possibly from a spell in the glass house. You heard the Chief Pusser. He'd be delighted to see me hanging up there from the yard-arm.'

O'Neill heaved a sign of relief. He could see that Perkins was as interested as himself in making a few bob on the side. 'Just you and me, Butch,' he whispered. 'Fifty-fifty. I'll keep the books right and you keep the stocks right. The Chief Steward'll pay cash on the nail on the last day of the month. You'll know exactly how many pounds of meat we've given him so there's no question of you being short-changed in any way. Okay? And I guarantee that the Chief'll never know a thing about it.'

The tannoy rattled and the bosun's pipe shrilled, followed by the call: 'Up spirits.'

'Jesus, is it that time already!' Butch squeezed O'Neill's arm. 'It's a deal,' he whispered. He turned to Marine Davies, still hacking at the beef. 'Okay, leave that, mate, we gotta get the bubbly up...'

They left O'Neill still standing with the menu in his hand. Something had just occurred to him.

'I don't believe this,' he said to himself as he checked over the meals for each day. 'He's put meat on again for the Friday dinner.'

The previous week when he took the draft menu to Paymaster Commander Humble for approval, the Paymaster had switched Tuesday's fish and chips to Friday and moved Friday's roast beef up to Tuesday.

'In deference to the Roman Catholics in the ship's company,' he had explained to O'Neill.

Recalled to the Royal Navy to fight Hitler's Germany, Paymaster Commander Humble found that he had little to do, apart from enjoying a few gins and tonics in the Wardroom, and a regular swig at the gin bottle he kept in his desk. As he saw it, his main function was to append his signature to every document that was presented to him. As these documents had already been scrutinised, cross-checked and initialled by either the Paymaster Lieutenant or the Supply Warrant Office, he didn't even bother to read them.

O'Neill was feeling pleased with himself as he headed back to the Victualling Office. It felt good to have one up on the Chief. Chief Hall and Hoskins were alone in the office.

'Chief,' O'Neill started, 'remember last week when the Pay-bob told you to put the fish and chips on Friday in deference to the Roman Catholic element...' The Chief nodded. 'Well, you've made the same mistake on this menu.' O'Neill held it out for the Chief's inspection. 'Lucky I noticed it before I took it to him for his approval....'

The Chief didn't even look up. He put his elbows on the desk and dropped his head in mock weariness in his two hands. He took off his glasses and cleaned the lens with his handkerchief. Then he withered O'Neill with what he liked to think was his most severe stare, reserved for junior supply assistants.

'O'Neill,' he said at last, his lips a thin line, 'you're a fucking wanker. D'you hear me?' He shook his head in his disbelief. 'Are you trying to tell me how to prepare the weekly menu? Are you?' O'Neill felt the blood rushing to his face. Hoskins paused in the middle of the long column of figures he was trying to add, the better to enjoy his mate's discomfiture.

'No, Chief.... but..' Chief Hall was enjoying himself. He was still thinking of his Slop Room back in Pompey.

'Lookit, O'Neill,' he said with exaggerated calmness, 'get this into your thick Irish skull - all Pay-bobs change the Friday menu to fish and chips. They do it every week in every ship in the fucking fleet. They have fuck-all else to do. It's the only thing they ever do. It's the only thing we allow them to do. Understand?'

O'Neill nodded. 'But what if he....?'

'Take no notice. He'll have forgotten this week that he did it last week. And he'll forget it next week that he did it this week. Okay? Don't take the poor old fart's only responsibility away from him....'

The door opened behind him and Supply Assistant White and Butch Perkins pushed their way in. Perkins had a gallon measure half full of grog in one hand and the rest of the brass measures in the other. O'Neill sighed. The Officer of the Day, a young midshipman, stood at the door and watched as Perkins emptied the grog into the sink. Then he nodded and left, his duty done. Perkins had the stopper into the sink before the midshipman's back was turned and then stood aside deferentially.

Chief Hall took a half-pint measure and filled it from the sink. 'God save the King,' he toasted, and drained the measure in one swallow. He threw the measure back into the sink and put on his cap. 'See to it, Hoskins, that a tot is kept for the Chief Cook.' Then, as the rum warmed inside him, he turned to O'Neill. 'Like a good lad, O'Neill,' he said genially, 'please take that menu down to the Pay-bob first thing after dinner and get his signature on it. And don't try to think any more, will you, there's a good boy. It obviously hurts your fucking head.' The staff tittered. The Chief shut the door. The others queued up, one by one, behind Hoskins, to drink the rum that was left in the sink.

Butch sidled up beside O'Neill. 'Godfrey's in your mess, isn't he?' O'Neill nodded. 'Ask him to come by and see me, will you, Jack?' he whispered. 'I need to have a word...'

Pay Commander Humble was in excellent form when O'Neill brought the menu to him in the afternoon. 'Ah, O'Neill, isn't it?' He indicated the spare chair beside his desk. 'Take a seat, man, take a seat.' He read down the menu. O'Neill watched him, fascinated, when he reached for his fountain-pen.

'You Irish, O'Neill?' O'Neill nodded, sighing. 'Roman Catholic, no doubt?' O'Neill nodded again and watched the circles being drawn around the Tuesday and Friday lunches. The smell of gin was quite overpowering. 'Tell the Chief that in deference to the Roman Catholic element of the ship's company, I suggest that it might be more appropriate to have the fish on Friday and the mutton on Tuesday.' He looked over his glasses at O'Neill. 'You'd agree with that, I'm sure.'

'Aye aye, Sir,' said O'Neill. He wondered about the kidneys on toast that were for breakfast on Friday and the corned beef and pickles that were for supper, but decided that it wasn't his place to get involved in a theological discussion on the matter. He stood up.

'Oh, one other thing,' Commander Humble said. He turned over the pages of his dairy. Every day was blank. 'Tell the Chief that I'd like him to accompany me on an inspection tour of the forward stores and the refrigerator rooms tomorrow afternoon at, say, 15.00 hours. We'll do the after stores on another day when I have more time. Not a stock-take, mind you, just a general inspection to make sure everything is ship-shape and Bristol fashion before we get out into the Atlantic...'

'Aye aye, Sir,' said O'Neill. 'Tomorrow afternoon, 15.00 hours, I'll tell the Chief.' He put on his cap and closed the door gently behind him.

Commander Humble sighed and reached into the drawer for the gin bottle. The sun was well over the yard-arm.

Chief Petty Officer Hall was not amused when O'Neill passed on the Commander's message but he had to restrain himself until Warrant Officer Smyth had left the office. Then he turned to O'Neill. 'You're quite sure he didn't say he wanted to take stock, just a general inspection...?'

O'Neill nodded. 'Wants to make sure that everything is ship-shape and Bristol fashion before we get out into the Atlantic, that's what he said, Chief.'

'The Atlantic, eh?' put in Hoskins. 'Could be the States we're going to...'

'Pipe down, Hoskins,' the Chief barked. 'I don't want any stupid buzzes starting from this office. Okay?' He turned back to O'Neill. 'Right, then, get the keys of Number 1 and 2 stores and the refrigerator rooms and you and I'll do a quick run-down there just in case.' He stood up. 'Chop, chop then. I haven't got all day.'

The bulkhead phone buzzed and the Chief lifted the handset. O'Neill took the keys from the key-cupboard and stood waiting at the door.

'Aye aye, sir,' Chief Hall said into the phone, and then covering the mouthpiece with his hand he whispered to O'Neill to carry on down to the refrigerator flat and he'd be along in a few minutes.

O'Neill went down the two ladders from the stokers' messdeck to the refrigerator flat and inserted the key in the padlock securing the air-lock door. He jumped when he heard a noise from the space behind him.

'What the fuck are you doing down here, Jack?' Butch Perkins's surprised voice demanded. O'Neill turned around, his mouth dropping open

'Jesus, I don't believe this,' he whispered. 'Jesus Christ!'

Writer Godfrey Wilkins was bent double behind the ladder, completely naked from the waist down, his underpants and trousers about his ankles. Butch Perkins hastily buttoned the fly of his trousers.

O'Neill came out of his shock when he heard the footsteps on the deck above. He nearly dropped the keys in his panic as he fumbled with the padlock. He got the door open at last.

'Quick, for Chris' sake,' he whispered urgently, 'that's the Chief Pusser on his way down to inspect the refrigerator.' He unclipped the heavy door of the Cool Room and held it open, a mist of cold condensation swirling around him. 'Inside, quick,' he gestured to them. 'Hide behind the cases of butter. He won't go in, he'll only look in...'

Godfrey started to blubber, his trousers leg caught in the heel of his shoe. Perkins grabbed him by the arm and pulled him, stumbling into the Cool Room. O'Neill shut the door and put on the two clips. He saw the Chief's shoes coming through the manhole in the hatch and tried to look composed.

'I - I've got the doors open for you, Chief,' he greeted, 'all ready for inspection...'

The Chief looked into the Cool Room and shivered. 'No duffel coats?' he asked.

O'Neill shook his head. 'Sorry, Chief. I keep two up in the Victualling Store. We bring them down with us when we open up in the morning, one for me and one for Butch. I'll bring them down with me when we do the inspection tomorrow.'

The Chief looked at him. 'Draw new ones from the Clothing Store,' he said. 'I wouldn't like to touch anything that fucking leatherneck might have been using.' O'Neill coughed noisily to drown a blubbering sound from behind the butter boxes. 'And make sure you have them here when the Pay-bob comes down. We don't want to freeze the balls off him...'

O'Neill shut the Cool Room door and opened the Cold Room. The Chief had a quick look in and seemed satisfied.

The tannoy squawked and the bugle sounded Stand Easy. The Chief shivered again. 'Okay, lock up here and we'll go and have a cup of tea. I'll meet you down on Number 1 store flat immediately after Stand Easy.'

O'Neill breathed a sigh of relief and sat for a minute on the ladder. That had been close. He ran up and stuck his head through the hatch to make sure the Chief was gone and then he went back and opened the air-lock door. He unclipped the Cool Room and switched on the light.

'All clear, you two randy bastards,' he whispered. 'The Chief's gone, you can come out now.'

Perkins came from behind the butter boxes followed by Godfrey, still trying to get his trousers up, his slim legs blue from the cold. His face was livid with rage as he knuckled at the tears running down his cheeks.

'You - you uncouth bollocks!' he spat at Perkins. 'You and your fucking golden rivet, I should have known what you were after..'

O'Neill turned to the crest-fallen Perkins. 'Golden rivet?' he asked. 'What's he on about? What golden rivet?'

Godfrey had his trousers up. 'I'll tell you what I'm on about.' He spat, his eyes on fire. 'This lecherous fucker spun me a yarn that every ship built for the Navy has one golden rivet, and he said that anybody who kissed it would be guaranteed never to drown - like being born with a caul over your face, only better, that's what he said...' He blubbered again. 'He brought me down here to show it to me but when I was bending down trying to see it he pulled my trousers down and – Jesus, I should have known what the bastard was after..'

He had his shirt tucked in at last. Perkins just stood there, a smirk twisting his lips. 'You didn't seem to mind very much...' Godfrey lashed a blow with the palm of his hand across the butcher's face.

'There! Take that, you stupid - stupid bloody butcher,' he snarled viciously. 'I should have known better than to associate with the likes of you.' He flounced up the ladder. 'I've a good mind to report you to Chiefie....'

When O'Neill was telling Hoskins what had happened in the refrigerator, he illustrated the incident by holding out his clinched fish with just the little finger drooping down.

'When Godfrey came out of the 'frige with his bollocks bare, his mickey was like that, all shrivelled up and miserable looking. I don't think it'll ever get back to normal. And I don't think he ever got round to kissing the golden rivet either...'

Hoskins laughed till he cried. 'Whether Godfrey's mickey ever gets back to normal or not shouldn't bother him,' he said. 'He'll only ever need it for doing his wee-wee...'

CHAPTER SEVEN

THE ATLANTIC

The convoy was four days into the Atlantic. O'Neill was slinging his hammock in the mess prior to getting his head down for the night. The door opened and an officer's steward stuck his head in.

'Supply Assistant O'Neill about?' he asked. O'Neill lifted his hand in acknowledgement.

'That's me,' he called, 'what can I do for you, mate?' The officer's steward grinned. 'If I had the time, I'd be delighted to let you do it for me, but unfortunately I haven't time right now.' He looked at his watch. 'Report at once to Sub-Lieutenant Booth in Cabin 17, Officers' quarters, port side. Okay?' He nodded and left.

O'Neill looked at Hoskins. 'Sub-Lieutenant Booth? What the feck could he want me for?'

Hoskins shook his head. Everybody on board knew of Sub Lieutenant's Booth. The Flying Irishman, he was called. When he was in the air they lined the walkways to watch in admiration as he threw his Seafire fighter about the sky in a bewildering series of aerobatic manoeuvres. Even Commander (Flying) was impressed at first. However, when Booth started flying the plane just a foot or two above the water, he came down heavily on the 20-year old pilot.

'But, sir,' Booth had protested, 'that's the only way I can appreciate the speed that I'm flying at. Way up there in the sky I might as well be on a bloody bike.'

O'Neill stood nervously to attention outside the open door of Booth's cabin. Booth was reading a letter and O'Neill saw that there was a pile of letters on his desk. He coughed. Booth looked up.

'Supply Assistant O'Neill, sir. I was told to report....'

'Come in, come in. And shut the door.' Booth searched through the pile of letters and extracted one. He handed it to O'Neill. 'Did you write this?'

O'Neill's face went red. It was the letter he had written to Norma. It had taken him hours to compose it and, Jesus, he had forgotten the fact that all letters leaving the ship were censored. There were things in there he wouldn't want other people to read. He nodded in embarrassment.

Sub-Lieutenant Booth swung his chair around. 'Do you realise you could be hanged for some of the things you said in there?' He took the letter from O'Neill and started reading from it: 'We're escorting a convoy across the Atlantic at the moment but we're going on to Bermuda and we should be there next week. I'm looking forward to that...' Booth's voice trailed off and he looked up at O'Neill. 'Passing confidential information about the movements of His Majesty's ships. What if this got into enemy hands? Have you any idea what sort of trouble this sort of thing would get you into? Have you?'

O'Neill shook his head, looking down at the deck to avoid Booth's glare. 'B-but, sir,' he stammered, 'by the time that letter is delivered in Liverpool, we'll be well gone out of Bermuda and be God knows where...'

'You Irish?' asked Booth. O'Neill nodded. Booth smiled. 'Look, O'Neill, as one Irishman to another, I don't like reading other people's letters but I get stuck with the job sometimes.' He lit his cigarette lighter and touched it to a corner of O'Neill's letter. 'I'm supposed to pass this to the Master-at-arms and you'd be faced with all sorts of charges and one thing is for sure, you'd never set foot on Bermuda.' He dropped the burning letter into the waste bin. 'So like a good man, off with you now and write that letter again and forget you're on a ship or where it's coming from or where it's going. Okay?'

O'Neill came to attention and saluted. 'Thank you, sir,' he said and turned to go.

'Oh, one other thing,' said Booth. O'Neill stopped. 'None of my business, of course, but this girl, Norma, are you in love with her?' O'Neill nodded, going red again. Booth grinned. 'Then for Christ's sake, tell her so, will you? Put a bit more passion into it. That's what she wants to hear from you, not about where this bloody carrier is going...'

The restless, heaving Atlantic swelled and tossed, lifting and dropping Pinewell's massive bulk as the carrier carved itself a spumy, white passageway through the long rolling breakers that reached up to smash relentlessly at her bows. Grey, menacing cloud hung all the way to the horizon. A cablelength away on Pinewell's port beam, a rusting oil tanker dipped deep, lifted and rolled. The searching sea swept in across her bows, and then rolled back in streaming torrents to flood down over her heaving stern. The convoy was steaming at a steady 18 knots.

Up in the rain-swept bridge, Captain Hastings worked his tall frame off the high steel chair welded to the deck, and walked stiffly across the gratings out onto the port bridge wing to stretch his legs. He tightened the duffel coat about him and jammed his cap down closer over his forehead as the wind sucked at him. He lifted his binoculars and focused one by one on the merchant ships stretched out in line astern hemmed in by escorting destroyers. The fact that he was the senior officer brought a rush of pride surging through him. The responsibility for the safe passage of the convoy lay firmly with him. Will I ever make Admiral, he wondered. Then he straightened his shoulders and went back to the weary loneliness and discomfort of his chair on the bridge.

In the Victualling Office, O'Neill was surreptitiously writing another letter to Norma. He had it hidden between the pages of the Wardroom Repayment Book. He was telling her how much he loved her and what a pity it was that they'd never got round to dancing together, and he was sure that she must be a wonderful dancer. Otherwise how could a slow foxtrot like Maria Elena be her favourite tune. Next time they met...

The bulkhead phone buzzed and Warrant Officer Smyth took off the hand-set. O'Neill saw him almost coming to attention in his chair.

'Yes, sir.' Smyth said. 'Yes, sir.' Three bags full, sir, thought O'Neill. 'Flying-helmet. Size 7. Of course, sir. No problem, sir.' Smyth hung up and turned to Petty Officer Taylor in the Clothing Section.

'That was Commander (Flying), Chief,' he said. 'One of his pilots, Sub Lieutenant Booth - wouldn't you know 'twould be that mad Irishman! - apparently he's mislaid his flying helmet...'

'Again, sir?' asked Taylor. 'That's the third one he's lost since he came aboard...'

'Anyhow, send him up another one to the Ready Room, right away. Size 7, and charge it to him this time, authority Commander (Flying), if he queries it. Okay? The bloody man's a nut, of course and he's been warned this time that he'll be grounded if he mislays any more Admiralty equipment.'

Petty Officer Taylor sighed and then noticed that O'Neill appeared to be writing a letter. 'You don't seem to be too busy, O'Neill,' he said sarcastically. 'Come down to the Slop Room with me and take the helmet up to the Ready Room. It'll give you something to do.'

In the Slop Room, Taylor showed him a cardboard carton full of flying helmets and told him to search through them for a size 7 while he made out the slop chit for Sub Lieutenant Booth. O'Neill located three size 7s and slipped two of them inside his jacket.

'Got it, Chief,' he announced, and showed the helmet to Taylor.

Taylor nodded and gave him the slop chit. 'Right then, take it up to the Ready Room and make sure Booth signs for it. Don't let the fact that he's Irish influence you.' He watched O'Neill climbing the ladder. 'Chop, chop then or you'll never get back to your letter writing....'

The Ready Room, on the gallery deck, was a bleak compartment, furnished sparsely with a blackboard, a steel cabinet and some uncomfortable slingback seats. It was here that the duty pilots, observers and air gunners sat around in bored groups, smoking, sleeping, gossiping or thumbing through magazines, but ever on the ready for the order to scramble. The rig of the day, as prescribed for the ship's company in Daily Orders, didn't apply in the Ready Room. Most of the occupants lounged around in battledress blouses with grey flannel trousers and woollen hats knitted lovingly by sweethearts, mothers or sisters.

On the whole, Sub Lieutenant Booth was thinking, sprawled on his chair, his eyes closed, it was a soul-destroying place to spend what might well be the last minutes of one's life. Rather like the prefects' room at Harrow, only less comfortable. He lit another cigarette morosely. It was beastly unfair of Commander (Flying) to threaten him with grounding if he lost any more equipment. A bloody helmet, for God's sake. It wasn't as if he had lost a kite, was it? Which, if rumour had it correctly, the bloody Commander himself had done more than once...

O'Neill pushed open the Ready Room door and his nose wrinkled. The hot, smoke-laden atmosphere in the cramped compartment was even worse than what they endured in the Victualling Office. There were seven air-crew personnel lounging about on chairs, nearly all of them smoking cigarettes. The two playing darts were puffing on cigars. Sub-Lieutenant Booth seemed to be asleep, his feet on a chair, his flying jacket lying across his lap. O'Neill stood beside him and coughed.

Booth's eyes opened warily and he peered up at O'Neill.

'Supply Assistant O'Neill, sir,' O'Neill introduced himself and proffered the flying helmet to the pilot. Booth sat up. 'I'm afraid you'll have to pay for this one, sir,' O'Neill apologised. 'Commander's orders...'

Booth took the helmet and tried it on. He smoothened the fine leather over the blonde curls and looked up at O'Neill. 'O'Neill. Of course. I remember now – the reluctant lover!' He grinned, looked around and lowered his voice. 'And fuck Commander (Flying) if you'll excuse the mutinous phrase, old boy.' He took off the helmet and dropped it on the deck with his flying jacket, and languidly scrawled an illegible signature on the slop chit that O'Neill handed him.

O'Neill checked to make sure the others in the Ready Room weren't paying any attention and then he slipped the other two helmets to Booth. 'I understand you lose 'em fairly easily, sir,' he whispered, 'and Commander Hunter has threatened to ground you if you lose any more equipment...'

Booth sat up, a smile spreading across his boyish face. He took O'Neill's hand in his. 'Damned civil of you, old man.' He grinned. 'We Irish must stick together, what?' His voice dropped to a whisper. 'You know my cabin, number 17 and if you should happen to drop by at about 20.00 when I come off duty, we could share a spot of gin together. I'd be honoured....'

The tannoy squawked and barked. 'Duty air crews report to Air Staff Officer.' Booth and the rest of the aircrews galvanised into action. Booth stuck the two spare helmets into his jacket pocket and was already gone before the voice on the tannoy barked again. 'Range one Swordfish and one Seafire on the flight deck immediately. Hands to flying stations. Stand by to fly off aircraft on routine patrol.'

O'Neill stood in the walkway keeping well clear of the crewmen hurrying to their stations, while at the same time trying to appear as if he were part of the sudden activity going on around him. It was the first time he had been on the island. From up there, the flight-deck looked huge, much longer than it did when he took his evening stroll with Hoskins, up and down, up and down till they lost count of the number of times they walked it.

The Deck Landing Control Officer had taken his position on the platform at the rear of the flight deck on the port side. He was dressed in a bright orange smock and had two orange bats tucked under his arm. He jammed his hat down firmly on his forehead as he watched the apparently feverish, but well rehearsed and highly controlled activity of the handling parties.

Signals jerked up to the yards and the carrier's deck tilted as she altered course into the wind. O'Neill watched, fascinated, as the handling party trundled the Seafire and the Swordfish to the after end of the flight deck. He saw Sub-Lieutenant Booth running, bowed into the wind towards his Seafire. A fitter gave him the thumbs-up sign and he clambered into the cockpit and adjusted the microphone to his mouth. The perspex canopy snapped into place and Booth was alone in a world of his own.

The Swordfish, J for Joker, was already rolling forward, the Australian pilot, Lieutenant Larg, still sucking at the butt of his unlit cigar, the helmets of the observer and gunner looming blackly in the rear cockpit. From the corner of his eye he saw Bats make a signal to the bridge and then the Affirmative broke from Pinewell's yard.

The Swordfish surged forward along the centre line, blue smoke and flame stabbing from its exhaust. It gathered speed, lurched over the curved bows to claw itself into the air, then tilting gracefully, it veered to starboard. Booth sighed in relief. No way would he fly one of those stringbags, especially when the weight of the two depth charges strapped underneath the fuselage brought its maximum speed down to less than 120 miles per hour...

The Aldis lamp stabbed again. Booth felt a surge of elation in his stomach when the powerful Rolls Royce Merlin engine growled into a roar at the touch of the throttle. The blurred figures on the bridge flashed by as the opening throttle sent him surging forward, weaving along the centre line, and then the deck vanished from under him and he zoomed high over the convoy's bobbing mast-heads. He retracted the wheels and eased back on the stick. Sub-Lieutenant Booth, a Wavy Navy pilot, was in the one place where he was genuinely happy - alone in the sky with K for Kate throbbing under him, the ocean far below.

'Hello, Leader, this is Kate. Do you read me?' He could see the Swordfish moving into the bank of cloud ahead.

'Hello, Kate.' He heard the moist chewing noise as Lieutenant Larg shifted the cigar from one side of his mouth to the other. 'I read you. Take station.'

Damned colonial, Booth grinned to himself as he soared high above the Swordfish. He could see the Aussie was still chewing morosely on the cigar. The sudden spurt of fire from the Leader's twin machine-guns startled him and reminded him that he too should test his guns. Better find out now if they were working rather than later when he might need them.

He eased back on the stick and soared up out of the cloudbank into the bright sunshine. He levelled off and pressed his right thumb firmly on the firing button on the joystick. The plane seemed to buck and vibrate when the two millimetre cannon and the four machine guns stabbed into fiery life. A short burst and he lifted his thumb. K for Kate was ready and willing. He eased back on the throttle, not wanting to get too far ahead of the Swordfish which he could see over to his starboard. He adjusted his goggles and settled back, easing the awkward parachute under him like a cushion. These routine patrols could be dreadfully boring.

At first glance Booth thought the white strip on the surface of the sea ahead was a breaking wavelet and he looked away. Then he realised that, if it was a wave, it was moving in a contrary direction across the line of long rollers that lifted and fell in a continuous shifting motion from horizon to horizon. He hauled the Seafire around to port to get a more direct bearing on it. Then he saw the dark grey conning tower shouldering the seas away as it heaved its way to the surface.

'Jesus,' he thought, 'a U-boat. I'm actually looking at a U-boat and its surfacing...' He brought the Seafire in a long swinging turn back and saw the Swordfish breaking from the bank of cloud below him.

'Hello, Leader.' Booth's mouth was suddenly dry and he licked his lips. Then he realised that he was whispering. He raised his voice. 'Hello, Leader. This is K for Kate. Do you read me?'

'Hello, Kate. This is Leader.' There was a pause. Booth knew that the cigar was being shifted again. 'I read you. In fact, I can fucking see you. I thought for a while there you'd gone home to your Mammy..'

Booth grinned. 'There's a sub surfacing dead ahead.' He had brought the Seafire full circle and the Swordfish was now on his port beam. They dropped down through the cloud-bank and he saw the submarine again, now on the surface, and arrowing its way through the wash that lifted around it.

Lieutenant Larg felt the acrid taste of chewed tobacco shreds in his mouth and realised that he'd bitten right through the cigar. 'Watch how's it's done, Kate,' he called, his Aussie accent cutting through the static. 'Am attacking now.'

Booth levelled off and watched the Swordfish moving purposefully towards the submarine. His teeth were clinched tightly. Hurry, for God's sake, hurry, he willed them, knowing that the old stringbag was almost bursting at her seams as she wallowed along at her top speed. Suddenly all Hell broke loose on the sub's conning tower when the Germans realised that they had unwittingly surfaced almost under the nose of a Swordfish which was now closing on their starboard quarter.

Stabs of green tracer reached out at the Swordfish tearing gaping holes in the fuselage. Booth ducked his head, his stomach heaving in nervous waves. He saw the depth charge plummeting down but even before the explosion came he knew that it had overshot the target and would cause little or no damage. The Swordfish lurched on and Booth could see the gunner swinging his twin barrelled machine-gun to send a stream of fire towards the sub's conning tower. Larg was crouched in his cockpit. On the submarine, he could see men scrambling from the platform back up the conning tower and Booth realised that she was preparing to dive. She'd be gone before the Swordfish could get into an attacking position again. This is it, he gritted. I've got to keep her on the surface.

The Swordfish swung on a tight turn, her port wing tilting down towards the waves. Larg too had seen the activity on the conning tower. Booth banked steeply and opened the throttle, watching the shape of the submarine looming larger across the racing propeller of the quivering Seafire. He was now flying as he liked to fly, just a few feet above the surface of the water flashing beneath him, a dazzling mist of flying spray and spume.

The sub's gun on the stand abaft the conning tower had suddenly come to life again. Nearer and nearer, Booth watched fascinated as the long streams of green tracer closed in on him. His eyes, clinched, blinked water. This is it, he thought, now or fucking never. He pressed his thumb on the firing button and saw his own tracer cutting long lines in the water, moving closer to the slowly moving submarine. His thumb was straining on the button. The sub loomed nearer. He saw the rending fire of his cannons and machine-guns closing in a concentrated apex on the sub's conning tower. Men tumbled from around the gun platform and jumped into the sea. He gunned the engine, veered sharply to starboard and felt the plane lifting violently as a huge explosion lifted the submarine almost out of the water.

Booth struggled with the stick fighting desperately to control the Seafire. He ducked when the Swordfish zoomed underneath him and only then realised that they had been flying almost on a collision course as they came at the submarine from its opposite quarters. He looked back. The Aussie's depth charge must have exploded level with the conning tower. The sub was already keeling over and men were tumbling from the tower into the sea.

'You trying to shoot me down or what, you stupid Pommy bastard?' Booth heard Larg's voice crackling over the intercom.

Booth grinned, sweat running coldly down his back. He sucked in gasping breaths of air. The elation flooded through him was almost suffocating. There was some damage to the port wing but it didn't seem to affect the performance of the plane. He gunned the engine and it surged forward comfortingly.

'You okay, K for Kate? K for Kate, you okay, cobber?' He detected a note of anxiety in the Australian's voice. He looked back. The U-boat was gone. There were men swimming around in the sea, others on inflated dinghies. He almost felt for them. Nobody was going to stop to pick them up. He felt suddenly weary.

'I'm okay, leader,' he called. 'And congratulations. Jolly good job of work for a colonial, I must say.' He heard Larg's relieved snort.

'Let's go home, cobber, and thanks for the free run you gave me there. The bastard never laid a finger on me. You earned your.... ' J for Joker's radio crackled and hissed and died. Booth called him up again but there was reply. He looked down at the Swordfish and saw Lieutenant Larg wave him on. He guessed that the Aussie's radio had been damaged. He waggled his wings in acknowledgement and then checked his compass and waited for the Swordfish to pick up course back to the carrier. The dashboard clock told him he'd been in the air for barely a half an hour. It must have been the longest half-hour of his life. A surge of elation at what he had accomplished in that short span of time flooded him. He climbed back up into the sun and snapped down the catch on his radio.

'Hello Tango, hello Tango,' he called the carrier. 'This is K for Kate. Do you read me?' There was a hiss of static.

'Hello K for Kate. I read you. What have you lost this time? Your bloody way?'

Booth detected the impatience in the Flight Commander's voice. This was going to be one up the arse for him. He tried to keep the elation out of his voice. 'One enemy U-boat sunk,' he reported. 'K for Kate and J for Joker returning home. No casualties but some damage to both planes. Nothing serious as far as I can ascertain. J for Joker's radio seems to be out of action...'

Within minutes, Booth could see the outlines of the carrier as he throttled back and dropped below the cloudbank. Pinewell was swinging away to prepare to land on aircraft. Booth flew around the convoy, swinging in a wide circle to allow the Swordfish to land on first. He could see the activity on the flight-deck as J for Joker made her approach, dropping down carefully and then flopping like an exhausted bird onto the deck. An arrester-wire grabbed the trailing hook and brought the Swordfish to a skidding stop. The walkways and gun turrets were lined with off-duty crew, waving and cheering. HMS Pinewell had drawn first blood.

On an impulse, he gunned the quivering Seafire low over the convoy and threw the plane into a Victory Roll as he thundered just above the lines of merchant ships. Cheering figures waved up at him. Booth was almost drunk with his pride. Commander (Flying) wasn't going to like this, but Booth was now so psyched up with his churning emotions that he no longer gave a damn. He clicked off his radio. Nobody was going to stop him now.

He turned in a long sweeping roll and came in astern of the carrier as if to land. He saw Bats frantically waving him off as the handling party tried to get the Swordfish past the safety barrier into the safe area. Booth grinned. His fingers tightened on the joystick, poised to throw the Seafire into another Victory Roll as he flew above the carrier.

O'Neill was still standing on the island walkway. The tannoy had told the ship's company of the destruction of the waiting U-boat. He, and everybody around him, had their hats off, cheering as they watched the two planes making their triumphant return.

Booth grinned when he saw the figures ducking in panic as the Seafire's dark, menacing shadow swept along the flight-deck. The Swordfish was in the safe area at last. Booth rolled his plane over in a Victory Roll, his port wing-tip just a few feet above the flight-deck. The safety barrier swung noisily up into place. There was a rending, tearing noise. Booth felt the jarring jerk as his port wing caught the steel safety net and tore off like cardboard. The Seafire bounced once and skidded in a wave of sparks and flame along the deck before diving over the sloping bows and vanishing into the heaving seas that reached up to engulf it.

'Release float,' came the urgent order from the tannoy. There was no sign of wreckage in the water. O'Neill watched hopefully as the float bobbed up and down, getting farther away from the carrier. Aldis lamps stabbed over and back between the carrier and the escorting destroyers. Commander Hunter, on the bridge wing, his binoculars focused on the carrier's wake, shook his head in frustrated fury. The damned fool, all those damned young fools who thought that the sky was their playground and the expensive planes their toys, would they always have to learn the hard way? Like Booth?

He realised that Captain Hastings was standing beside him. Their eyes met briefly and Hunter shook his head, confirming what Hastings had already decided. There was no point in organising a search for Booth. He was dead. There were more important matters to be attended to.

'Port watch to defence stations,' the tannoy boomed. 'Supply Assistant O'Neill report to the Victualling Office at the double.'

O'Neill jumped and hurried down the crowded walkway. Everything was back to normal. He tried to finish the letter to Norma but his heart wasn't in it. He'd write it some other time....

Chapter Eight

Bermuda

'....beautiful beaches tinged with pink coral sand, lush vegetation and brilliant blooms, a temperature that never falls below 59 degrees Fahrenheit or rises above 85. Bermuda is called an island but it is actually made up of 140 separate islands in a 22 mile curve, just two miles deep at its widest point..'

Captain Hastings, relaxing in his chair on the bridge, thought the Medical Officer was laying it on a bit thick. All he'd asked him to do was warn the ship's company about the dangers they were likely to encounter in Bermuda, what with the cheap rum and loose women and suchlike that were, apparently, readily available. There really was no need to go on like a bloody travel agent...

Surgeon Commander Fielding moved his mouth closer to the tannoy microphone and paused dramatically. As always when he gave these talks, he felt that, far from being on the bridge of a ship, he was on the stage of the Old Vic, firmly held in the spotlight, his enthralled audience hanging on his every word. And they were. On every messdeck, in the recreation space, in the aircraft hangar, in the engine room, officers and ratings alike listened to the soft Scottish accent outlining the beauties and joys that lay ahead of them in this magic island of Bermuda.

Hoskins had put aside the letter he was writing to Pearl. O'Neill was already in his hammock, swaying to the movement of the ship as Pinewell steamed at a steady 20 knots through a sea that seemed to get smoother and bluer as they approached Bermuda. He pulled on a cigarette, his copy of Men Only resting on his naked chest as he hung, spellbound, on the doctor's words. He was going to like Bermuda; he could feel it in his bones. He closed his eyes and pictured all those lovely dusky maidens, their shapely hips gyrating provocatively, their plump breasts swaying in rhythm to the heady beat of the Calypso music. He had seen them in the films. This was going to be a dream come true.

.... 'and I have no doubt that some of you are already dreaming about going ashore in Hamilton to dip your penises into places where I wouldn't put my walking stick,' intoned Commander Fielding, warming to his subject. O'Neill opened his eyes with a guilty start. 'Then you'll rush back aboard and expect me and my staff to cure you of the pox, or syphilis or whatever disease you've picked up.'

Captain Hastings nodded his approval. That was more like it. This was the sort of stuff he wanted to get across to the crew - not all that bullshit about reefs of pink coral and a subtropical garden paradise. The doctor paused again. 'I have been authorised by the Captain to warn you that anybody who gets himself a dose in Bermuda will be confined to the ship until such time as we arrive back in England, and the Captain assured me that he doesn't care how long that will be....'

Captain Hastings nodded again, watching a school of flying fish flopped across the blue water on the port beam. Commander Fielding finished with a flourish.

'French letters are available in the Sick Bay. Make sure you draw one before you go ashore - one per man, per night. The Sick Berth Attendant will keep a record of the names of all those who draw them. And God help anybody who arrives back on board with a dose if his name isn't on that list.' Another dramatic pause. 'Enjoy yourselves in Bermuda..'

O'Neill's gaze met Hoskins's. Then he looked up despairingly at the deckhead. 'Enjoy yourselves,' he repeated. 'How the Hell does he expect us to enjoy ourselves after that? He'd put you off eating in Bermuda never mind anything else..' The tannoy clicked again.

'One other small point I should warn you about,' came Commander Fielding's voice again.

'Sweet God,' groaned O'Neill, 'If there's any more, I'm not even going to go ashore in this kip...'

'There's a large naval dockyard in Bermuda,' continued the doctor, 'and most of the workmen came out here from Britain with their wives and families some years ago. Now, they are, more or less, native Bermudians. But a lot of their daughters don't like it here. They feel restricted. They want to get back to Britain and their only hope is to marry a British sailor. Some of these girls are so desperate that they'll go to any lengths to trap you into marriage. Need I say more ? Watch out for it.'

Dora Atkins was such a girl. Tall, blonde and beautiful, she was a junior receptionist in the Hydro Hotel, just a short ferry-ride across the bay from Hamilton. Her parents came to Bermuda twenty years ago and she had been born on the island. Now, more than anything in the world, she wanted to get back home to the England she had never known. The news had spread like wildfire around the island that there was an aircraft carrier in the dockyard in Ireland Island, on the north shore.

Dora had seen the sailors, resplendent in their white linen uniforms, swarming ashore from the liberty boats in Hamilton. And, joy upon joy, she had struck gold on the first night at a tea-party thrown by the Christian Women's Guild to welcome the visiting sailors. She had charmed and delighted Supply Assistant Jimmy O'Neill, and, this evening, he was coming to take her out.

Madame Dupont, the owner of the hotel, came out of the dining room and approached Dora's desk, looking pointedly at her watch.

'What time did you say this - this young man of yours was calling?' she asked in her throaty French accent. A lot nearer to fifty than she would ever admit, Madame Dupont was haughtily beautiful, her dark hair pinned in a severe bun at the nape of her neck, her curvaceous figure still tall and erect. Dora was convinced that the sexy French accent was totally affected. After all, it was thirty years ago since she came to Bermuda. You'd think she'd have acquired a Bermuda accent in all that time.

Dora smiled brightly at Madame, hoping that nothing had gone wrong. This, unfortunately, was her late-night duty week when she was supposed to be at her desk until midnight and then serve in the bar until it closed at 4 a.m. Madame had kindly agreed to take over Dora's duty until midnight to enable her to go out with O'Neill.

'He's coming for me at six o'clock, Madame,' she said, glancing at her watch, 'in about twenty minutes time.'

Madame nodded, a small smile twisting her full lips. She patted Dora on the shoulder.

'Off with you then, *cherie*,' she said, 'and get yourself ready for your young man. I'll look after the desk.' She sighed. 'The things I do for *amour, oh la la!*' She waggled her finger at Dora in mock severity. 'But like Cinderella, be sure that this sailor boy brings you home here by midnight, and not a minute after it, you understand. There's no way I can handle the bar until four. At my time of life, one daren't miss out on one's beauty sleep.'

O'Neill, accompanied by Hoskins, arrived at five minutes to six. In accordance with Daily Orders, they were dressed in their No 6s, single-breasted white linen jackets, fastened at the neck, the rank insignia on their sleeves in vivid blue, linen trousers lightly starched and stiffly creased to razor-edge sharpness. They had white covers on their caps and wore white leather-soled canvas shoes.

Madam Dupont was impressed when they walked hesitantly into her foyer - especially by the tall, fair-haired boy who she immediately decided was Dora's escort. Hoskins' admiring glance took in the outdoor swimming pool, the flower-packed, beautifully manicured lawns and the spacious patio where some of the guests, all Americans, were sitting sipping their aperitifs before visiting the dining-room.

'Jesus, Paddy, how do you always manage it?' he whispered enviously. 'This is a grand little place you've got here.' O'Neill grinned. Madame Dupont left the desk and came to meet them, her hand outstretched in greeting.

'Welcome, *messieurs*,' she beamed, her gaze never leaving O'Neill's face. 'You are very welcome.' She shook their hands in turn. 'I am Simone Dupont, the owner of the Hydro. Which of you handsome boys is Dora's escort?'

Hoskins noted that she was still holding O'Neill's hand.

'I am,' said O'Neill. He squeezed her hand gently, his eyes flirting with her. Suddenly he was thinking of Norma Perkins. God, he thought, she looks so like her even though she's much older. It must be the way she has her hair tied in a bun like Norma. 'And if you'd care to join us, I'd be delighted to have you...'

Madam Dupont pouted her lips provocatively. 'Oh, you bold, bold boy!' she giggled. 'Whatever would Dora say if I agreed to such an outrageous suggestion...' She linked arms with the two of them and led them towards the bar. O'Neill was surprised to find that she was nearly as tall as himself.

They saw Dora standing at the foot of the stairs watching them. She was dressed in a silk floral frock that clung to her willowy body emphasising every sexy curve. Her blonde hair hung down to her shoulders. O'Neill's approving look made her heart beat a little faster.

'Ah, *cherie*,' Madame Dupont said to her, 'I was just going to get these handsome sailors of yours a drink. You'll join us, yes?'

Dora hesitated, looking at her watch. 'I don't think we have time, thank you, Madame,' she said, her gaze on O'Neill. 'The ferry will be leaving in a few minutes. I really think we should go.'

O'Neill sensed the hostility in Dora's voice and wondered what was wrong. Madame Dupont squeezed his arm.

'Perhaps, some other time....?' she smiled at him. O'Neill bowed. Dora grasped his arm possessively and almost dragged him to the door. Stupid bitch, Hoskins was thinking to himself, I could have done with a few free shots of good Bermuda rum...

'What's the rush?' O'Neill whispered to Dora. 'We have plenty time...'

Dora's lips tightened. She looked back. Hoskins was shaking hands with Madame Dupont.

'Don't think I couldn't see what that French tart was up to,' Dora said 'She was trying to pick you up, couldn't you see that?' She looked back over her shoulder. Madame Dupont was still laughing with Hoskins. 'And she old enough to be your grandmother, for God's sake...'

Hoskins saw the smile in Madame Dupont's eyes harden to a steely glint. Like a lot of sailors, he was slightly deaf, an affliction brought about by exposure to the constant hum of generators and fans aboard ship. He wasn't quite sure what Dora said but he guessed that Madame definitely had heard. And, whatever it was, she hadn't liked it...

Madame Dupont watched the three crossing the patio to walk down to the ferry and then went back into the hotel foyer. For fully a minute she stood looking at herself in the full-length mirror behind the desk. Old enough to be his grandmother, indeed! Jealous little bitch! Oh well... She nodded approvingly at her reflection in the mirror and smiled a satisfied little smile. There was much life and much passion in that shapely body yet...

It was nearly ten minutes to midnight when O'Neill and Dora got off the ferry and hurried up the path to the brightly lit hotel. The dance had been very enjoyable and Dora had responded positively to his caresses and advances. He felt he was on to a good thing. Now, unfortunately, it was nearly midnight. Like Cinderella, he had to catch the last liberty-boat from Hamilton, and that left in half an hour. Not much time to accomplish anything. And he'd set out with such high hopes.

Dora, for her part, was quite happy at the way her plans for romance and eventual marriage were taking shape. The Pinewell was off to sea again tomorrow for further working-up exercises and the buzz was, Jimmy told her, that they'd be back in Bermuda again in about a week. That would be time enough to let O'Neill have his way with her. No point in letting him get it too easily. She stopped in the shelter of an oleander tree and pulled him against herself, her arms encircling his neck. He held her close and she could feel his hardening urgency as he kissed her. His hand felt her breast and she squeezed against him.

'I love you, Jimmy,' she said softly against his lips. He let his tongue touch hers.

'I love you too, darling,' he whispered. His hand slid down her body but she pulled it back.

'Not now, darling,' she whispered, her voice full of promise. 'I don't want to spoil our first time by rushing....' She pushed her hips against him and felt him bulging. 'We must go in now,' she said, pulling away and smiling up at him. 'Madame will be waiting. She warned me not to be late...'

Madame Dupont was sitting at the desk when they arrived in the foyer.

'How punctual you are, *cherie*.' She smiled, looking at her watch. 'I agreed to work until midnight so you still have five minutes to spend with your *beau*. I won't deprive you of that. Go and sit in the lounge - you won't be disturbed.' She smiled archly at O'Neill. He grinned back.

'I'd love to do just that, Madame,' he said, 'but, unfortunately, I've got to catch the liberty-boat from Hamilton at 12.30. It's that or sit on the pier till the 7 o'clock boat in the morning...'

Madame Dupont looked from O'Neill to Dora, her brow furrowed quizzically. 'Sit on the pier all night?' she asked. 'Oh dear, oh dear, that would be terrible. That is completely out of the question.' She paused and considered. 'I know,' she said, 'why not stay here in the hotel tonight? If you don't have to be on board till morning, why waste tonight? Stay here.' She looked back at the keyboard. 'Number 48 is vacant. You can sleep there.'

Dora looked at O'Neill. It was obvious from the expression on his face that the prospects of a good night's kip in a comfortable bed was appealing. Madame Dupont handed Dora the key of Number 48.

'Show your young man where Number 48 is.' She smiled. 'I'll put you down for an early call at 6.30.' She waved an admonishing finger at O'Neill.

'And don't you try any tricks up there, sailor boy. I've had a long day and it's way past my bedtime. Dora's on duty until four. After that....' She looked from one to the other, her voice trailing off conspiratorially.

Dora blushed. O'Neill grinned happily. Hoskins was right. This was, truly, a nice little place he had here...

He fell asleep straight away. Though Dora had been coy about it, he was fairly certain that she'd come straight to Room 48 as soon as she came off duty. The night was sultry and the silvery light from the huge moon hanging in the sky threw warm shadows around the room. Outside the frogs and crickets chirped in the trees. The night was alive with promise. O'Neill was lying flat on his back, the bed covers thrown aside on the floor. He was naked.

He didn't hear the door opening, nor did he wake when the lights flooded on. Madame Dupont, dressed in a shimmering silk dressing-gown stood beside the bed and looked down at his naked body. She put a bottle of rum and a bottle of coke on the dressing-table and picked up the french letter, still in its packet where O'Neill had placed in readiness. She dropped it distastefully into the waste basket. Then she returned to the bed. She smiled and took his limp penis between her thumb and forefinger and waggled it delicately. O'Neill sighed in his sleep and tried to turn over. She squeezed his penis gently again. He opened his eyes and looked around in surprise, not sure where he was. Then he saw the tall figure bending over him, the caressing fingers feeling him, and he sat up.

'Madame - Madame Dupont,' he stuttered, his hands going down in embarrassment to cover his nakedness. 'It was hot - I threw the covers off...' He looked at his watch. 'It's not time to get up already, is it ?'

Madame Dupont smiled and pulled his hands away. 'He looks so tired, poor thing,' she said, pointing at his penis. 'What's his name?'

O'Neill was fully awake now. He looked at her in surprise and then he grinned, his embarrassment diminishing. He thought for a second or two. 'Mickey,' he said, at last. 'Or if you want to be formal, Madame, Michael.'

'I don't wish to be formal. Jimmy O'Neill.' She smiled. 'So do please call me Simone and, yes, I'll call him Mickey.' She paused for a moment. 'Yes, I do think I like Mickey but I'm rather disappointed that he doesn't stand up in the presence of a lady.'

O'Neill sat up and looked at his limp penis. Then he reached out and attempted to pull at her dressing-gown. She stepped back.

'I'll tell you what, Simone,' he said, 'I'll bet he'll stand up if you let him have a little peep at you-know-who.' He pointed between her legs. 'What's her name, by the way?'

It was Simone's turn to be taken aback. 'How dare you, you bold boy?' she pouted. She pulled her dressing-gown more tightly about her. 'My Suzy doesn't speak to strange men. Especially strange men called Mickey...'

She went to the dressing table and filled one of the glasses half full of rum and added some coke. She handed it to O'Neill and then put coke in the other glass for herself. O'Neill gulped at the rum and coughed.

Madame smiled down at him and switched on the radio. 'Radio Bermuda plays very nice dance music at this hour of the night,' she said. 'I thought, perhaps, you'd like to dance with me?' O'Neill looked at his clothes piled on the chair and reached to get them.

Simone pushed the chair away. 'All you'll need are your shoes.' She picked them off the floor and handed them to him. She sat on the bed in silence as he put them on and laced them.

The man on the radio said that he was now going to play a slow fox-trot, Maria Elena. Oh my God, thought O'Neill remembering the night in the YMCA in Liverpool. Norma is haunting me tonight. Why couldn't it be some other song?

Simone took O'Neill's hand and pulled him out of the bed. They melted into one another's arms and he knew immediately that Simone was an excellent dancer. Her thin silk dressing-gown was soft against his naked body. He sensed she had nothing on underneath. Her cheek was resting against his, her warm breath touching his face. As they danced slowly around the room he kissed her. She stopped and braced herself against him, her lips burning. She could feel his penis wedged between them.

'Oh Jimmy O'Neill, you naughty boy....' she whispered. O'Neill's hands slid down her back, covering the cheeks of her bottom and pulling her close as she arched back, pressing against him, her arms around his neck.

'Mickey says he is most uncomfortable where he is,' he whispered. 'He wonders if he could come in to Suzy's place and then you and I could carry on dancing...?'

Simone pouted her lips and then nodded. 'Suzy says that Mickey can come in her place as often as he likes.'

They were in front of the full-length mirror on the wardrobe and O'Neill twirled her around to face it. He stood behind her, his arms around her waist. She lifted her arms up and held his face in her hands. Her breasts jutted out stretching the silk of her gown, her belly a voluptuous silky mound. Their gazes locked in their reflection in the mirror. O'Neill's hands slid down and untied the knot in her belt. Gently, in time to the haunting music of Maria Elena, he slowly, teasingly, opened her gown. Her long legs, teetering on high heels, were slim and deeply tanned, her thighs strong and firm, crowned by a curly rosette of dark hair.

'You are beautiful, Simone,' he whispered .

The gown was fully open and he let it slip down between them. His hands caressed her body, touching between her legs, sliding up to her breasts and back down again. She twisted around to face him and they locked together. She reached down and then standing tall, she slipped him inside her. ' Oh my wonderful, wonderful Jimmy.' She sighed. 'Why did you take so long...?' Her arms were around his neck. Slowly, almost fearfully, they moved to the caressing rhythm of Maria Elena.

'....Maria Elena, say that we will never part. Maria Elena, take me to your heart.' O'Neill sang the words softly to her, his body swaying with hers, feeling every curving movement of her thighs and breasts. 'A love like mine is great enough for two...'

She stopped suddenly and jerked, her arms tightening around him. O'Neill looked down at her. Her eyes were closed, her face aglow. She stiffened again.

What's wrong?' he whispered. She opened her eyes and smiled up at him.

'Suzy sneezed,' she said. Then she giggled throatily 'In fact, she sneezed three times.' O'Neill hugged her closer. 'Bless her,' he whispered. They swayed to the music. Then it was his turn to stiffen and groan.

'Is something the matter, *cherie*?' Simone asked. O'Neill's hands were pulling the plump cheeks of her bottom, forcing her body hard up against his. He opened his eyes and kissed her.

'It's Mickey,' he whispered. 'He's just done a terribly bold thing.'

Simone giggled. 'I know,' she said softly, 'I felt him doing it. He spat right into Suzy's eye. But Suzy says she doesn't mind. In fact, *cherie*, she says Mickey can do it as often as he likes. She just loves it...' She backed towards the bed and fell into it, O'Neill on top of her, firmly held inside her.

She sneaked a quick look at her watch. It was half past two. They had one and a half hours before Dora came off duty. She hugged O'Neill close. 'Suzy says she's ready every time Mickey is..'

Dora too kept looking at her watch impatiently as the hours and minutes crawled slowly by. She had worked herself into an almost feverish pitch of passion as she waited for four o'clock. She had already decided that she couldn't let this opportunity pass. Tonight, she would give her all to her darling Jimmy O'Neill and, hopefully, one day he would get her off this wretched island and take her back to England as his bride. The radio in the bar played Maria Elane and Dora whispered the words to herself, dreaming that she was in Jimmy's arms...

At five minutes past four she was outside Room No. 48, her heart racing in anticipation. She wasn't a virgin but she had never actually been in bed with a man. She ran her fingers through her hair and slowly opened the door. She slipped inside. The room was in darkness but she could see the bed and the shadowy outline of the figure lying on it. She stepped out of her shoes, then lifted her frock over her head and dropped it on the floor. Her bra followed and after a moment of nervous indecision she pulled down her panties and stepped out of them. She stood in the darkness and lifted up her breasts with her two hands in a massaging caress. She touched nervously down to the soft mound of hair between her legs. Then, satisfied that she was ready, she reached out and switched on the lights.

Dora's breath gasped out of her. Oh, Jesus, she thought, the bloody bitch, the bloody Froggy bitch! O'Neill was lying flat on his back, stark naked except for his canvas shoes. The empty rum bottle was still clutched in his hand. The top of his penis was painted a bright vivid red and Dora recognised the colour immediately - Madame Dupont's lipstick. The french letter, which was blown up like a balloon, was tied to his penis by a length of white thread. O'Neill snored gently. Dora pulled her frock over her head and stepped into her shoes. She picked up her bra and her panties and, tears streaming down her cheeks, she fled down the corridor to her own room.

Madame Dupont heard Dora's door slam and smiled. She stretched luxuriously between the cool sheets and let her hand slip down between her legs, gently massaging herself.

'Dearest Suzy,' she whispered happily, 'dear little Suzy, you may be old enough to be Mickey's grandmother but tonight you gave him a night that he'll never forget...'

Suzy sneezed again. Simone slapped her gently. 'You naughty, naughty girl,' she whispered, 'that's the tenth time tonight...' Then she fell asleep.

Chapter Nine

Malta

The confident buzz that Pinewell would return to Bermuda after a few days of working-up exercises had been wrong and O'Neill didn't know whether he was glad or sorry. When he crawled out of the bed in the hotel and saw his shocked reflection in the mirror, his eyes sunken, his penis scarlet with the blown-up french letter dangling from it - oh my God! He grinned in spite of himself as he juggled with the figures in the Wardroom Repayment Book. That Madame Dupont was one very sexy lady. He felt himself ruefully - he was still tender from the scrubbing it had taken to remove the lipstick. He tried not to think of Dora.

Captain Hastings had put paid to all the rumours when he addressed the ship's company the day after they sailed out of Bermuda.

'We will shortly,' he told them, pride bubbling in his voice, 'be playing a vital role in one of the greatest fleet operations of our country's naval history. The island of Malta is on the verge of collapse, bombed, starved, cut off from essential supplies of fuel and food...' He paused to get their undivided attention. 'HMS Pinewell will be part of a fleet which will escort the convoy getting those supplies through to save the island and change the course of the war. This operation has been code-named Pedestal. We will pass through the Straits of Gibraltar at 22.00 hours on August 10th...'

'Operation fucking Pedestal!' groaned Chief Hall as the Victualling office staff listened to the Captain's announcement over the ship's tannoy. 'That's just about all I need at my age.' He looked balefully at Hoskins and O'Neill.

'If he's so anxious to win himself a medal why couldn't he just take you two fucking heroes along with him and leave the rest of us in Bermuda ? The three of you are well matched - fucking stupid!'

Operation Pedestal started out for Pinewell with trials out in the Atlantic. Accompanied by the aircraft carriers, Eagle, Indomitable and Victorious, they now came under the command of Rear-Admiral Lyster. The four capital ships, and their escorting destroyers, ploughed in convoy through the heaving Atlantic seas, manoeuvring in-line abreast, then in line astern, flying high and low cover patrols, and practising night take-offs and landings. When Admiral Lyster was satisfied that the squadron was ready for the task ahead, he hoisted the order to join the main force assembling west of Gibraltar.

O'Neill and Hoskins, standing on the walkway below the flight-deck, watched in awe as the fleet and convoy formed up in the cruising formations which would be employed after they passed through Gibraltar and approached the dreaded Narrows.

'Jesus,' said Hoskins, 'I didn't realise we had so many warships left...'

There were 14 merchant ships in the convoy. They sailed in four columns, three-quarters of a mile apart. An anti-aircraft cruiser led them and another cruiser covered their rear, with two more on their flanks. The battleships Nelson and Rodney took station on each side of the rear ships in the convoy with two destroyers providing close anti-aircraft cover on either beam.

O'Neill counted at least twenty destroyers in an arrow-shaped protecting screen surrounding the convoy at a distance of about two miles. There were two more in reserve picking up at the rear to fill any gaps that might occur if a destroyer had to leave the screen to check out submarine contacts. Altogether, there were 66 warships protecting the convoy of just 13 merchant ships and one tanker.

All through the day, fleet and convoy carried out emergency turns, zigzag patterns and other group movements while planes from the carriers made dummy attacks from all quarters to provide stark realism to the manoeuvres. As sundown started to crimson the western skies over the waters of the Atlantic, Pinewell's Marine bugler sounded Action Stations and Hoskins and O'Neill joined the well-rehearsed exercise as all personnel hurried to their battle stations. Hoskins, O'Neill and writer Godfrey Wilkins, with Regulating Petty Officer Jones in charge, formed the crew manning Y magazine which supplied 4" shells to the after turrets.

'Chop, chop then, you lot,' Regulating Petty Officer Jones barked as the three of them came scrambling down the vertical steel ladder into the magazine. The Regulating Petty Officer was the Master-at-arms assistant, and known in naval parlance as the Crusher. He was looking at his watch. 'You'll have to get here a damn sight faster than that. Jerry isn't going to wait for you, you know...'

'Turret to magazine,' interrupted the voice-pipe. 'Report your state of readiness.' Petty Officer Jones put his mouth to the pipe. 'Magazine to turret,' he replied. 'Magazine crew present and correct.'

'Send up 10 starlight shells, Chief' he was instructed, 'and stand by.'

Y Magazine was an L shaped compartment, 30' long, with tubular racks reaching from deck to deck-head all loaded with 4" shells each weighing about 70 lbs. Hoskins went to the farthest point down the magazine and with a special key unclipped a shell and drew it out about four inches from its container. O'Neill's job was to pull it clear, hoist it on to his shoulder and dash to the lift where the Crusher was waiting. The lift was a continuous moving belt with steps every three feet. O'Neill placed the shell on the lift platform and the Crusher, timing his actions precisely, pushed it on to a step in the belt. This carried it up five decks to the turret. Wilkins and O'Neill alternated as 'donkeys' humping the shells from storage rack to lift, constantly harried by the Crusher egging them on to faster effort.

When the starlight shells were dispatched to the turret, there was nothing to do but wait. O'Neill and Hoskins flopped down on the deck at the end of the magazine, their backs to the racks, their eyes closed. Godfrey stretched languidly full-length on the deck, a bath towel spread under him, his cap a pillow under his head and read a volume of poems. The Crusher pretended to sleep but, through half-closed eyes, he ogled Godfrey's long, brown legs in his tight shorts.

The atmosphere in the magazine, combined with the claustrophobic effect of the narrow passageways, was quite intimidating. Though wearing only light shirts, shorts and canvas shoes, the magazine crew sweated freely. Apart from the odd snippets of information gleaned over the voice-pipe and tannoy, they were in a world of their own far divorced from any action that might be going on above them as escort and convoy headed for Gibraltar. Thirty minutes later the bugler sounded the dismissal from action stations

At 22.00 hours on the night of August 10th, the convoy and escort, in three groups, passed through the Straits of Gibraltar into the Mediterranean.

Admiral Syfret sent a signal to all ships under his command. Chief Hall, O'Neill and Hoskins were in the Victualling Office when Captain Hastings read the Admiral's encouraging words over the tannoy.

'....during the next few days all ships will be in the first and second degrees of readiness for long periods. When you are on watch be especially vigilant and alert. For that reason, when you are off duty, get all the sleep you can. Every one of us must give of his best. Malta looks to us for help. We shall not fail them....'

'Stupid bollix,' said Chief Hall, filling himself out a large tot of rum from the jar he kept locked in the drawer of his desk. Pointedly, he didn't offer any to Hoskins and O'Neill.

Actions Stations sounded at 6 am on the morning of the 11th and Y magazine's crew scrambled back down the ladders to their post, sleep still screwing up their eyes. Even in the pre-dawn darkness, the Med air was warm and sultry.

'Stay alert then, you three,' Petty Officer Jones warned them when they flopped down on the deck and tried to get back to sleep. 'This isn't an exercise any more. The Jerries and the Wops are out there and I have no doubt they're waiting for us...'

Nothing happened. Half an hour later, the bugler sounded the all clear. After a hasty breakfast, O'Neill and Hoskins returned to more or less normal life in the Victualling Office. They spent the next two hours supervising the supply of 50 cases of corned beef to the galley. For the next few days the staple diet for the ship's company would be corned beef sandwiches and 'pussers kye', a thick nourishing chocolate drink on which, as Hoskins put it, 'you could trot a fucking mouse.'

'Up Spirits' came and went without incident. After eating their corned beef sandwiches, Hoskins and O'Neill went up to the starboard walkway to get some fresh air and smoke cigarettes. The fog that had blanketed the sea as they passed through the Straits had lifted. A stiff east wind whipped up little white wavelets that tossed across the surface of the sea making it difficult for the look-outs to distinguish which was a wavelet and which might be the searching white trail of an approaching torpedo. To the north, a thick band of white cloud hung over Majorca above the horizon. To the south the coast of North Africa lay below the hanging mist. The beleaguered island of Malta was still 550 dangerous miles to the east. The sirens boomed and escort and convoy zigzagged 40 degrees to port.

'It's too quiet,' said Hoskins, dragging deep on his cigarette. His voice was almost a whisper. 'It's too fucking quiet...'

O'Neill shaded his eyes from the sun. High above them three Seafires in formation, droned across the convoy. 'What the fuck are you grumbling about?' O'Neill demanded. 'Maybe they don't know we're here. Maybe it won't be as bad as we thought...'

✢ ✢ ✢ ✢ ✢

Kapitanleutnant Herman Beck, commander of a 500-ton German submarine, was one of four German U-Boats and eighteen Italian submarines already in place cruising along the expected route of the convoy. Eight of the Italian submarines were spread out in formation to keep watch for the convoy which their Intelligence Services had warned them was about to enter the Mediterranean.

Their orders were explicit. Each submarine captain had been informed of the times when the convoy would be attacked from the air. Just before the air raids, any subs in the vicinity of the convoy were to show themselves briefly, at a safe distance, hoping to entice the escorting destroyers to leave the screen, thus reducing the fire-power of the convoy. During and after the attacks, they were to close on the convoy while it was bunched together. This action, hopefully, would increase their chances of sinking the ships with their torpedoes.

On the island of Sardinia, 150 German bombers, with 50 fighters to cover them, were waiting patiently for their quarry to arrive within striking distance. At airfields in Sicily, 130 Italian bombers, 90 of them torpedo bombers, with fighter cover of 150 machines were also lying in wait. And already, one of the Italian subs had sighted the convoy early that morning and reported its position as being 60 miles south of Ibiza in the Balearic Islands.

The role of the four German U-Boats, two to the north of the expected route and two to the south, would have been of particular interest to the optimistic O'Neill. They had been specially detailed to penetrate the destroyer screen and sink the aircraft carriers.

Kapitan Herman Beck's U-Boat was lying at a depth of 90 feet. He was thinking of his wife, Irma, back in Oderhaven. In her last letter - he touched it in the pocket of his jacket - she told him that she had closed the flat temporarily and had gone to live with her father and sister, Renata. Her father owned the Hotel Kaiser just opposite the railway station in the centre of the town. Guests were few and far between but, at least, she felt she was of some help and the work kept her occupied.

'Propeller noises approaching from the west.' The voice snapped Beck instantly from his reverie. The U-Boat came alive with feverish activity. Tanks were blown until it reached periscope depth.

'Up periscope!' Beck stiffened when the masts of a destroyer, two miles away, loomed into view. He moved the periscope in a wide sweep and it filled with the large bulk of an aircraft carrier travelling, he estimated, at about 20 knots.

Before he could identify it, four tall spouts of water reared up to twice the height of the carrier's main-mast as a salvo of four torpedoes exploded deep in her hull. Beck didn't wait. He gave the order to dive deeply. Even as he changed course to take up a new station to the east and ahead of the convoy, he heard the crash of the depth-charges exploding. He smiled grimly. First blood to his classmate, Rosenbaum in U.73. Now there were only three carriers and the convoy had already lost 25% of its air-cover.

'Jesus!' whispered O'Neill in awe, fear gripping like a clenching fist in his stomach. Less than half a mile away HMS Eagle, clouds of dark smoke fanning out behind her, was dragging slowly to a stop. She was already tilting to a 50 degree angle and men were tumbling into the water from her decks.

Action Stations sounded. With one last look at the doomed carrier, O'Neill followed Hoskins in a rush to the magazine. With sirens hooting, the convoy and fleet swung sharply in a 90 degree turn to protect themselves from the silent, hidden enemies lurking in the bright waters of the Mediterranean.

Kapitanleutnant Beck had taken up his new station. It was now five o'clock in the evening and he knew that the convoy would be experiencing the first of a series of concerted air attacks from Sicily and Sardinia. Even at this depth the sub's crew could feel and hear the muffled thuds of exploding bombs. A less daring Kapitan would have laid low in the safety of the deep, but not Beck. He gave the order to blow tanks and take the U-Boat up to periscope depth.

After each successful patrol, U-Boat Kapitans were awarded a silver goblet. After the seventh patrol, the set was completed by the award of a silver tray to hold the six goblets. Unfortunately, Beck mused, not many U-Boat Captains lived long enough to complete the set. This was his seventh patrol and if his luck held he would soon be returning to Oderhaven. Irma had the six goblets sitting on the piano. Hopefully, he would be bringing her the tray...

'Up periscope.' Beck's eyes swept across a broad stretch of gently heaving ocean. His pulse quickened. About two miles away on his port bow the outline of an aircraft carrier loomed in the periscope mirror. He quickly counted five destroyers and a cruiser in a protective screen around her.

The noise of churning propellers drew nearer and a destroyer loomed into his view. It was over a mile away and presented no danger. Beck watched as a pattern of depth-charges flew out from her decks and exploded in the water. He swung the periscope to pick out the carrier again, noted her course and took the sub down to a depth of 90 feet. He ordered full speed ahead on a course that would close him on the carrier. So far so good. His luck was holding.

The crew of Y magazine had been closed up at action stations for over four hours. O'Neill's shirt clung to his back in the sweaty heat of the magazine. He had lost count of the number of shells that he had humped from the racks to the lift. All he knew was that they seemed to be getting heavier. Now and again, they got word either over the tannoy or from the turret voice-pipe that enemy planes were mounting another attack. They, however, two decks below water-line, were in a world of silence.

'Jesus,' said Hoskins when, for a fraction of a second, Pinewell's 23,000 tons bulk seemed to come to a shuddering halt and then surged forward again, 'what the fuck happened then?' O'Neill was thrown against the racks and the shell he was carrying on his shoulder clattered on the deck. The lift whined to a halt. O'Neill felt his shoulder gingerly.

'What's happening up there,' the Crusher shouted into the voice-pipe. All four waited impatiently.

'Turret to magazine,' said the voice-pipe calmly, 'as you were. A bomb exploded on the flight-deck. We've lost power in the turret but everything seems to be okay.'

The Crusher mopped his sweating face with a towel. 'Stand easy, then, and grab a rest,' he ordered. O'Neill and Hoskins flopped down on the deck by the lift. Wilkins went to the back of the magazine, his book of poems under his arm. The Crusher followed him.

Kapitanleutnant Beck brought his U-Boat back up to periscope depth and had a look around. So far they seemed to have escaped detection. The fleet's look-outs and asdic operators were probably distracted by the constant air attacks or else density layers of cold water were shielding the U-Boat when the pinging fingers of the asdic probes reached down to search him out. There were three destroyers between him and the carrier he had identified as the Pinewell. He noted with satisfaction that fires were burning on her flight-deck. The attacking planes had obviously scored a hit. He dived again and started his attacking run. It was now or never.

Ten minutes later he brought the sub up to periscope depth. 'Stand by to fire forward torpedoes on my order,' he called. He waited and watched the convoy moving slowly across the circle in his periscope. The image of the carrier was moving towards the crossed wires in the sight. 'Stand by,' he called again.

'I don't like it,' whispered Hoskins to O'Neill. 'I don't like it, it's too fucking quiet.' With the lift was no longer working, an eerie silence, broken only by the hum of the fans, had descended on the magazine.

'Don't start that again, for God's sake,' pleaded O'Neill. The red warning light in the phone beside the lift flickered. Hoskins lifted the handset and put it to his ear. 'Y Magazine,' he said.

'Stand by for the Gunnery Officer.'

Hoskins mouthed to O'Neill to fetch the Crusher. O'Neill pulled himself to his feet and padded down the passageway. He came back immediately, his face puckered in disbelief.

'You're not going to believe this,' he whispered.

Hoskins eyebrows lifted. 'Believe what?'

'It's the Crusher,' O'Neill said.

'What about the Crusher?' Hoskins demanded impatiently. 'Is he alright?'

O'Neill nodded. 'Oh, he's fine. I'm not too sure about Godfrey, though...'

'Godfrey? What's wrong with Godfrey?' Hoskie's voice was getting narky.

O'Neill grinned. 'The - the Crusher's stuck up him.'

'Oh Christ!' Hoskins looked at the handset not sure what to expect next.

There was a buzzing noise and the Gunnery Officer's voice sounded faint. 'Clear the magazine,' he ordered, his voice taut. 'Secure all watertight doors and hatches and report with your crew to the Fire Control Officer on the flight-deck.'

'Aye, aye sir,' said Hoskins. He put back the handset. 'Clear the magazine,' he shouted. 'Secure all watertight doors and hatches. Report to the Fire Control Officer on the flight-deck.' He was already half way up the vertical ladder exiting from the magazine, O'Neill close on his heels.

'Clear the magazine!' They heard the Crusher's hoarse shout as they reached the next deck. 'Everybody out!'

Hoskins looked back at O'Neill and shook his head. 'Did you hear that?' he asked. 'Everybody out and he the only fucker in...'

They scrambled up three ladders and had reached the well-deck level when the salvo of torpedoes exploded deep inside Pinewell. O'Neill was close behind Hoskins on the ladder. He clung desperately to the rungs when the stricken ship lurched as if a giant dagger had been thrust into its side. Above his head Hoskins was almost through the manhole in the hatch when the blast of the explosion snapped the heavy steel cover shut and, like a snaring gin-trap, it closed on Hoskins's left ankle. O'Neill heard him scream. The lights went out and the emergency lamps flickered on immediately.

Panic choked O'Neill. He reached up in the semi-darkness and pushed the cover off Hoskins's foot. Warm blood dripped onto his face when he eased the smashed foot through the hatch opening. Then he climbed through. Hoskins was lying in a heap on the hatch. O'Neill turned him over.

'Come on, Hoskie!' he shouted. 'Come on, we gotta get the hell out of here. We're nearly there.'

Hoskins eyes flickered but he didn't move. O'Neill grabbed him under the arms and dragged him along the deck to the door leading out to the open well-deck. He stepped out and panic choked him again when he saw that it was already awash. And, for the first time, he heard the din of the battle, which had raged all afternoon.

Bombs were exploding all around the convoy and spurts of flame reached up from the guns of the fleet, tearing away the darkness which was spreading across the Mediterranean. The piercing scream of dive bombers deafened him.

Out of the corner of his eye he saw a flash light up the sea when a torpedo slammed into one of the merchant ships. The blast sent him staggering against the bulkhead. A nervous dribble of urine ran down his leg.

'Abandon ship!' The tannoy just above O'Neill's head blared. Deep in Pinewell's bowels he heard a creaking sound and crunching explosions as watertight compartments were torn apart by the rush of water pouring through the gaping holes torn in her side. Strangely, almost with dignity, Pinewell was sinking squarely, no tilting decks, no diving bow carving deeply into the Med where she had served so briefly.

O'Neill could see bobbing heads already in the water. With a gasping grunt he heaved Hoskins's body onto his shoulder and stepped over the rail. He held on for a moment with one hand and then stepped forward. The warm water closed about him, relieving him of his mate's dead weight. He rolled onto his back, keeping Hoskins's face clear of the water with one hand, and started swimming desperately to get as far as possible from the ship before she could suck them down to join her in her lonely grave. Klaxons and sirens hooted and the convoy desperately zigzagged again through 90 degrees. His Majesty's Ship Pinewell and her survivors were suddenly alone. The battle had moved on. An eerie silence settled around them.

They didn't see Pinewell going under but they felt the pulling rush of water and they heard the last gurgle as the sea closed over her. Hoskins had regained consciousness but was barely able to fend for himself.

The night was calm and a bright moon lit up the sea. It was Hoskins who saw the bobbing carley float some twenty yards away and shouted to O'Neill. They struggled to it and pulled themselves aboard.

'Sweet God,' gasped O'Neill, 'I was beginning to think we'd have to swim all the way to Gib.'

There was no reply from Hoskins. O'Neill bent over him and saw that the effort to get onto the float had been too much for him. He had fainted again. He examined the damaged ankle and felt his stomach turn. The lacerated flesh was black and blue and the ankle was swollen to twice its normal size. He opened the lace and removed the canvas shoe as gently as he could. Even so, Hoskins gasped in pain and his eyes flickered open. O'Neill tried to cradle the foot between his knees to keep it out of the water in the float.

'How bad is it, Paddy?' Hoskins gritted through clenched teeth. 'It feels as if every shagging bone in there was smashed.'

O'Neill thought it looked that way too but he tried to sound cheerful. 'Let me put it this way, Hoskie,' he said, 'you won't be going dancing at the South Parade Pier for a month or so...

Hoskins lay back to ease the pain in his throbbing ankle. He sat up suddenly, wincing in agony. 'Look!' He was pointing at a dark shape floating in the water just ahead of them. O'Neill shaded his eyes and saw the flash of a white face bobbing up and down. Even in the half light he recognised the red bushy hair.

'It's Taffy,' he whispered, 'it's Taffy Jones, the canteen manager.'

He reached out as far as he could and grabbed Taffy by the collar of his shirt.

'Okay, Taffy bach,' he called, 'I've got you. Welcome aboard. I was beginning to think that Hoskie and meself were the only two....'

His voice trailed off and he nearly got sick again. Half of the Canteen Manager's head had been blown away and he could see the white of what was left of the brain. He let go and the body started to drift away.

'No, Paddy, for Chris' sake, don't let him go. Hang on to him.' Hoskins was almost screaming. O'Neill reacted involuntarily and grabbed the canteen manager by the sleeve of his shirt. Hoskins was pulling himself painfully across the float.

'He's dead, Hoskie,' O'Neill whispered, 'can't you see ? He's dead. Half his head's blown away...'

Hoskins leaned out over the side of the carley float and held the body steady by its arms. He turned to O'Neill. 'Search inside his shirt, Paddy.' They were both whispering now. 'Hurry, for fuck's sake,' Hoskins grimaced, his face white with pain. 'I won't be able to hold him much longer. See if he's got anything inside his shirt.'

Mystified, O'Neill slipped his hand inside the canteen manager's shirt. He shuddered when he touched the cold skin of the hairy chest. His fingers closed on something. It was round and cold and sausage-shaped and there were several of them. He looked at Hoskins, puzzled. Why would Taffy carry sausages under his shirt, for God's sake? He drew out one of them and examined it in the light of the moon. 'Oh my God,' he whispered in disgust and dropped the object as if it had burnt him. It was a french letter and it had something inside it - something stiff and about six inches long. It was knotted at the end. O'Neill's eyes were wide with horror. He glared at Hoskins, still struggling with Taffy's body.

'Go on,' he shouted angrily, 'I suppose you're going to tell me that Taffy's like that other depraved pal of yours in Portsmouth, that mad fucker who collected the royal shits...' He looked at the object floating in the water inside the float and picked it up gingerly between his thumb and forefinger. 'So what does Taffy collect, eh?' he demanded. 'Royal pricks?'

Hoskins looked at him, open-mouthed. He reached back with one hand and picked up the discarded french letter and held it under O'Neill's nose. 'The Chief was right about you, Paddy,' he said, 'you're thick. That's your trouble, you're fucking thick. Can't you see? That's money! The takings in the canteen. NAAFI money. You don't think Taffy was fool enough to keep it locked up in the safe, do you?'

O'Neill took the french letter and examined it more closely. Hoskie was right. It was a roll of notes protected in the waterproof french letter.

'Hurry, for God's sake, Paddy,' grunted Hoskins, 'I can't hold poor old Taffy much longer. Get the rest of the money out of his shirt...'

There were twelve french letters in all. Each roll of notes had been inserted lengthways, a breath of air blown in to make it buoyant and the end knotted. The Canteen Manager had, in effect, made himself a lifebelt of NAAFI money.

O'Neill watched Taffy's body float away. Then he leaned over the side of the carley float and was violently sick. Hoskins watched him. Then he too started vomiting. When they finally got their breath back, they sat in silence, their feet in a foot of water on the timber grating. The french letters were bobbing like sausages in the float. Hoskins gathered them together and proffered them to O'Neill.

'You'd better hide these inside your shirt now, Paddy,' he said. 'We wouldn't want to let anybody else see them...'

O'Neill shook his head and pushed them from him. 'No bloody way, Hoskie,' he said, horrified. 'You keep them. I wouldn't touch them. No way.'

'But you've got to, Paddy,' Hoskins pleaded. 'When we're picked up I'll be taken straight to the Sick Bay and stripped. You'll just be given a change of clothing and you'll be able to hide them until we can divide up later on.'

O'Neill reluctantly accepted the logic of Hoskins's argument and slowly packed the french letters inside his shirt. Then he was sick again. Hoskins, his face drained from exhaustion, had drifted into semi-consciousness.

Long fingers of light touched the eastern horizon. Soon it would be daylight. O'Neill closed his eyes. The carley float bobbed gently in the water.

He wondered if there had been many survivors. He hadn't seen many in the water after Pinewell sank.

'Ahoy the float!' The call brought O'Neill awake with a start and he looked around. His heart leapt in sudden fright and he cringed down. Hoskins was still out for the count. The dawn light made everything coldly stark. A U-Boat was on the surface, twenty feet away, towered over the tiny float. Two sailors were manning the machine-gun abaft the conning tower and it was aimed directly at O'Neill.

'Ahoy the float.' Kapitanleutnant Beck's voice was impatient. 'Sit up, man, I can see you.' He realised that the crouching figure in the float thought the U-Boat was about to open fire and he gestured to the two sailors to return to the conning tower. O'Neill sighed in frightened relief and sat up. The officer was now alone in the conning tower. His gaze met O'Neill's and he smiled. O'Neill forced a smile in return.

'Your shipmate, he's injured?'

O'Neill nodded. 'His ankle is smashed but he'll be okay.'

'You were on the Pinewell?' the officer asked.

'Yes, sir,' O'Neill said. And then, getting suddenly cocky, he added, 'Was it you sank us?'

The officer shrugged and O'Neill thought he sighed. 'It is war. To survive is the main thing.' He swept around the horizon with his binoculars. The sun was up. He looked at O'Neill again. 'You'll be picked up before the day is over. Many ships will be passing back to Gibraltar. Unfortunately, I cannot wait for them. I too suffered some damage.' He smiled and saluted. 'Auf Wiedersehen. I wish you luck.'

O'Neill lifted himself up and returned the salute. 'Thank you, sir,' he called, 'and the best of luck to you too.'

Kapitanleutnant Beck was right. The cruiser, HMS Sudsbury, her bow and f'xle twisted by a direct hit from a German dive-bomber, picked up Hoskins and O'Neill. On the afternoon of August 13th, they were back in Gibraltar.

Chapter Ten

Norfolk VA

Norfolk, Virginia - Shit City to every blue jacket in the United States Navy - was O'Neill's first experience of America and things American. Nearly three weeks had elapsed since he and Hoskins were plucked from the Med by HMS Sudsbury. Now, looking out over Norfolk's sprawling dockland and the city beyond, he wondered whether he'd made the right decision when he agreed to stay on the Sudsbury. Proudly, he fingered the new gold anchor on his left arm. Leading Supply Assistant O'Neill! That, of course, was an unexpected bonus.

A few days after HMS Sudsbury tied up to the wall in Gibraltar, O'Neill felt sufficiently recovered from his ordeal to sample whatever delights the Rock might have to offer. He was half way across the brow, resplendent in his brand new uniform, when a call came over the tannoy ordering him to report to Supply Chief Petty Officer Mullins in the Victualling Office. For a few seconds he debated with himself whether to ignore it and carry on ashore but then decided against. It might be some word about Hoskie who had been carted off to hospital when they docked.

'Ah, so you're O'Neill!' Chief Mullins indicated the chair beside his own and invited O'Neill to sit down. 'Are you okay now? It was fucking rough up there....' O'Neill nodded, wondering what this was going to be about. Mullins hardly wanted to exchange views with him about the run to Malta. A worried little pulse started beating in his forehead. Jesus, it couldn't be about the twelve french letters of NAAFI money he'd hidden in the bottom of his new kit bag. He hadn't even had the opportunity to check out how much money they contained.

The Chief took a rum jar out of the cupboard in his desk. He lifted his eyebrows in question. O'Neill nodded and Mullins poured out generous measures into two cups. He handed one to O'Neill. 'To your continued good health and mine,' he toasted and drained his cup in one gulp.

'I'll drink to that any day.' O'Neill grinned and drained his too. Mullins poured out two more. There's a catch in this, O'Neill thought. No Chief Pusser gives good rum away like that without a reason.

Mullins sipped at his drink, mustering his thoughts. 'How long have you been in the navy?' he asked.

O'Neill did a quick calculation. 'Two and half years,' he said, 'nearly all of it at sea, and after that run to Malta I'll be looking for a shore job.' He sipped at the rum. 'I'm being transferred to the base here tomorrow and I wouldn't object to a spell in Gib.'

'I see,' said Mullins. He gazed thoughtfully into his cup. 'My Leading Supply Assistant was injured and they tell me he'll be in hospital for months. I need someone experienced to replace him. The sprog assistant I've got is only just out of training and he knows sweet fuck-all about everything.'

O'Neill shook his head. 'Sorry Chief,' he said, 'and anyhow I'm not a Leading Supply Assistant.' He pointed at his bare left sleeve. 'I haven't even applied to take the exam.'

Mullins nodded. 'I know, I know, but let me give this to you straight, and keep it strictly between ourselves, okay?' O'Neill nodded. 'This tub is going to the States for repairs and we'll probably be there for five or six months. Now, without a replacement for my leading supply assistant, I'll be in the shit right up to here.' He held the cup above his head. 'I'm putting this proposition to you because I know that after two years at sea you must know your way around.' O'Neill nodded again. The Chief took a deep breath. 'I've talked to the Pay Lieutenant and if you volunteer to stay on the Sudsbury he'll be quite happy, on my recommendation to promote you straight away to the rank of Leading Supply Assistant - no exams, no fuck-all!' He emptied his drink.

'Could you get a fairer offer than that, I ask you? And I'll tell you something else for nothing - you'll find that I'm an easy man to work for, not like some bastards I've had to work under myself, down the years.' He held out his hand. 'How's about it, Leading Supply Assistant O'Neill, will we shake on it?'

'O'Neill hesitated for a second and then they shook hands. He hoped he wouldn't regret this when the effects of the rum wore off.

'You off ashore now chasing a bit of Spanish?' Chief Mullins asked. O'Neill nodded. The Chief sighed. 'When I was your age I was like that. Nowadays I get a lot more satisfaction from a good shit.'

Next morning, O'Neill was brought before the Captain and on the Paymaster Lieutenant's recommendation he was promoted to Leading Supply Assistant. That afternoon Sudsbury slipped its moorings and put to sea. Next day, O'Neill took the twelve french letters from his kit bag and, in the privacy of the bedding store, he checked their contents. Then he checked and rechecked, his fingers trembling. They contained £4,560 in rolls of notes of various denominations.

'Sweet God,' he whispered, hardly able to believe his luck. He did some quick calculations in his head. 'That's more than the Navy'll pay me over the next 40 years - even at my new rate.' He thought of Hoskins in the hospital in Gibraltar. Then he put the rolls of notes back into the french letters. He nearly got sick when he put the first one to his mouth to blow into it. It felt as if he was tasting the acrid smell of Taffy's dead body. He closed his mind and finished the distasteful task.

'We're fucking millionaires,' he whispered reassuringly to himself. 'Hoskie and I are fucking millionaires.' A sobering thought struck him and he added, '- if I can manage to stay alive long enough to get the money back to Blighty...'

Quickly overcoming his revulsion, he packed the clammy french letters inside his vest and for the next ten days as they ploughed across the Atlantic he endured them there till they reached Shit City. No way was he going to lose that money if they were torpedoed.

One of the first tasks Leading Supply Assistant O'Neill performed for Chief Mullins was to type a certificate stating that the items of stores listed hereunder were being written off having been destroyed or damaged by enemy action when the Sudsbury's Lamp Room was struck by a bomb on the way up to Malta.

'I don't believe this,' he said to Supply Assistant Shorty Smith who was alone with him in the Victualling Office. 'The shagging Lamp Room aboard this tub must be as big as an aircraft hanger.' The list of stores destroyed had run to four pages. 'There must have been damage to some other storerooms. You couldn't get this lot into ten Lamp Rooms.'

Shorty grinned. 'You won't believe this either but don't ever let on to the Chief that I told you,' he said, his voice dropping to a whisper. 'Every morning after we left Greenock with the convoy to Malta the Chief'd come into the office and sit down there on his chair and then he'd bless himself and start praying.' Smith solemnly made the sign of the cross and bowed his head reverently. 'Please, God, send us a bomb,' he'd whisper. 'A small bomb will do, or even a near miss, but please, dear God, send us a bomb or I'll finish my days in the fucking glasshouse. Thank you, God. I know you won't let me down...'

'I don't believe it!'

'I told you wouldn't, but it's true, every word of it.' Smith assured him. 'I reckon the Chief made a packet on some deal or other when we stored ship before we left Greenock.'

O'Neill read down the list again. Definitely somebody had made a packet if this lot was being written off. The Chief came into the office and flopped into his chair. O'Neill handed him the finished certificate. He read it, nodding solemnly. 'That sure was a fucking rough trip to Malta,' he said. 'Fucking rough.' He initialled the certificate and handed it back to O'Neill.

'Like a good man, take it down to the Paybob and get him to sign it,' he said. 'The sooner we get that lot written off the ledger the better. You can't be too careful about these things, I always say. No, indeed, you can't be too careful.' He rolled himself a cigarette and lit it. 'Oh, by the way, if the Paybob asks you where the Lamp Room is, tell him it's up at the pointy end of the ship where the bomb exploded.' He winked at O'Neill. 'He's a wavy navy man, you see, and he doesn't know very much about anything.'

Shorty Smith sniggered. The Chief glared at him and then turned back to O'Neill. 'Our Paybob was a dressmaker, I understand, before he joined up but he has a lot of influential friends in high places and that's how he got a commission. So don't be surprised when you see the sewing machine in his cabin and the rolls of cloth he brought aboard with him. He's still at it, making fucking dresses, keeping his hand in, he says.' He shook his head and looked up despairingly at the deckhead. 'Takes all types to fight a war, I always say, takes all types....' O'Neill decided that this wasn't the right time to ask any questions.

The Chief hadn't been strictly accurate when he described Paymaster Lieutenant Keith Davidson as a dressmaker: he was, in fact, a dress designer who, before the war, was internationally recognised as one of the rising stars in the *haute couture* world of fashion. He signed the certificate, without comment, and handed it back to O'Neill. He smiled when he saw O'Neill staring in fascination at the blonde female figure lying stark naked on the bunk.

'She's not real, unfortunately.' He grinned. He reached out and pulled off the wig, exposing a shining wax pate. 'It's only a dressmaker's dummy. I'm sure the Chief has already told you that I design ladies' clothes - the fact seems to amuse him somewhat. I use Sylvia here for fitting the garments as I make them up.' He reached under his desk and handed O'Neill a portfolio of drawings. 'Know anything about ladies clothes?' he asked, 'apart possibly from trying to get them off....?'

O'Neill smiled. He thumbed through the sketches. They were, he decided, the weirdest collection of female garments he'd ever seen and nobody he knew would dream of wearing clothes like these. He tried to think of something polite to say. 'They - they're very nice, sir,' he said at last, 'very nice, indeed, except....'

Lieutenant Davidson laughed and put the drawings back under the desk. 'Except that, like the Chief, you think I'm a bloody weirdo. Yes?'

'Oh, no sir,' stammered O'Neill, totally taken aback. It was beginning to dawn on him that maybe Lieutenant Davidson wasn't quite the half-wit that Chief Mullins thought he was. 'It's just that, well, I don't know anybody who'd wear stuff like that...' He opened the cabin door. Lieutenant Davidson was eyeing him up and down.

'How tall are you?' he asked. O'Neill hesitated, puzzled. 'Five foot, ten, sir, in my socks. Why?'

'Ever do any modelling? Clothes, I mean.'

O'Neill laughed, slightly shocked at the question. 'Modelling? Me, sir? You must be fucking joking.' He felt himself going red. 'Sorry, sir but....'

'That's alright, old man.' Davidson stood up and got a tape measure from his desk. 'D'you mind if I take a few measurements - just the waist and hips? The chest doesn't matter - I have a padded bra that you could wear.'

O'Neill panicked for a moment when he remembered the french letters but by standing stiffly to attention and pressing his palms to his ribs he kept them high up under his vest. The lieutenant deftly ran the tape around his waist and then his hips.

'34 waist and 38 hips,' he said. 'Ideal! In our fashion house we cater for the fuller figure woman, you see....'

O'Neill was getting flustered. 'Sir....' he started.

Lieutenant Davidson pushed the dummy back against the bulkhead and sat on the edge of the bunk. He indicated to O'Neill to close the cabin door and sit down. O'Neill did so reluctantly. This was all getting a bit above his head.

Davidson smiled. 'Look, O'Neill,' he said, 'stop looking so bloody frightened, will you? Whatever you or the Chief might think of clothes designers I'm not a weirdo and I'm not a brown hatter and I'm not even vaguely interested in your arse except, possibly, in the size of it from a fashion point of view. Understood?'

O'Neill relaxed slightly. 'May I smoke, sir?' he asked nervously taking a packet of cigarettes from his pocket. Davidson nodded but refused to take one himself. 'Now, war or no war, I'm putting together a small collection and this unexpected trip to America opens up all sorts of possibilities for me and my career - as a designer, I mean.' He ran his fingers through his dark wavy hair. 'I'll never be a naval officer, not even if the bloody war goes on for ever. But I do have good connections with the fashion world in New York and if I have this lot put together by the time we get there, it could make a tremendous difference to my prospects when this bloody war is over. You understand?'

O'Neill nodded, not understanding at all. 'But - but, sir, what's all this to do with me? I mean, what can I do about it...?'

Davidson changed his mind and took one of O'Neill's cigarettes. 'What I'm asking - asking, mind you, let me emphasise that - is that you'd come down here when I want you and just fit the dresses for a minute or two...' O'Neill stood up. 'No, please, O'Neill, hear me out. All you have to do is stand there and move your arms about so that I can see how my creations look on a live figure.' He jabbed a finger at Sylvia's bottom. 'She's dead. She doesn't bring my clothes to life. She's....' He sighed. 'Okay, O'Neill, I know this all sounds weird to you, you having no experience of the fashion world, but all I'm asking you to do now is consider my proposition. And remember what I said - I'm no weirdo and I'm not interested in arse. Okay?'

O'Neill's gaze met Davidson's in a steady stare. 'But why me, sir? I mean, you could have asked Shorty White or - or any of the staff...'

Davidson shook his head. 'Oh, don't think I haven't considered them, I have but you've just said it - Shorty - he's too bloody short to be a model. And Leading Supply Assistant Jones, the man you replaced...' He shook his head sadly. 'A barrel. A fat little barrel. The same goes for Leading Writer Gordon.

But you? You're just right. You're proportions are perfect for what I have in mind. What do you say?'

O'Neill dragged on his cigarette. He thought about his promotion and how it had come about. Then he made up his mind. What the fuck had he to lose? 'Okay, sir.' He grinned. 'I'll try anything once and I do own you a favour.' He touched the new gold anchor on his sleeve. 'So whenever you want me, give me a shout. But for God's sake, please don't tell anyone...'

Lieutenant Davidson stuck out his hand. 'You won't regret this decision, old man. And of course, you'll be paid the going rate - in cash.'

They shook hands. O'Neill picked up the signed certificate from the desk. Lieutenant Davidson took it and looked down the list of stores destroyed or damaged by enemy action. He shook his head thoughtfully. 'That Lamp Room must have elastic bulkheads,' he said.

Seven times in the next ten days, O'Neill got the word from Lieutenant Davidson to attend at his cabin for fittings.

Each summons meant a trip to the Bedding Store to remove the french letters from under his vest. He hid them beneath a pile of mattresses, with a silent plea to God not to send a torpedo before he got back.

In the privacy of Davidson's cabin, he stripped to his underpants, buckled on the padded bra and then donned whatever garment Davidson was working on. Lastly he put on Sylvia's wig.

'Jesus,' he whispered the first time, his face scarlet, 'I hope nobody ever comes in here and catches me like this.' He lifted up his jutting breasts with his hands. 'I'd never live it down.'

Davidson smiled, his lips tight holding pins. 'No danger of that,' he said. 'Anybody who's not on watch will be sucking gin in the Wardroom.' He turned O'Neill around. 'Stand up on your toes,' he instructed, 'as if you were wearing high heels.' He tucked the garment in at the waist and secured it with pins and then stood back. 'Turn around slowly and lift your arms above your head.'

O'Neill twirled gracefully, the soft material swirling about him. He felt himself getting half-hard. Davidson made some more adjustments and nodded his approval. 'Though I say so myself, O'Neill, that garment will wow them in New York. Yes, siree!' He eased the wig from O'Neill's head. 'Okay, just let me slip you out of that one and we'll try one more. That'll do us for this session...'

Back in the Bedding Store. O'Neill fingered the two pound notes that Davidson had insisted on paying him. Over a week's wages for ten minutes embarrassment, he thought happily, and I actually enjoyed it. He slipped the french letters inside his vest and spread them around evenly.

'You know something, Jimmy O'Neill,' he whispered happily, 'you're a fucking walking money-making machine. A whore in Lime Street couldn't make money as fast as you can...'

The night after they arrived in Shit City, O'Neill and Leading Writer Gordon decided to find out what the United States of America, and particularly, Norfolk, Virginia, might have to offer. They boarded the bus outside the dockyard and were lucky to get seats half way down the aisle, as hundreds of dockyard workers swarmed out through the gates.

Two stops later a black girl climbed aboard. O'Neill's eyes lit up. She was tall and shapely and the tight white frock seemed to cling caressingly to every curve of her flesh. She stood beside their seat in the aisle, one hand lifted high to hold the leather strap, her full breasts bulging tantalisingly just above O'Neill's head. He could smell the warm perfume of her body. When the bus lurched forward she swayed trying to hold her balance and her belly touched against O'Neill's arm. He elbowed Gordon.

'Have you no manners at all?' he whispered. 'Stand up and give the lady your seat.'

Gordon ignored him. 'You give her yours,' he suggested. 'You're on the outside.'

O'Neill sighed and stood up. He turned on his most winning smile, his eyes looking soulfully into hers which were a beautiful shade of brown, big and widely spaced with long sweeping lashes.

'Please,' he said, 'may I offer you my seat?'

She stared at him for a second and then pointedly turned her back. He felt himself reddening. Everybody on the bus was watching, some smirking, some embarrassed for him. He decided that perhaps she didn't speak English.

'My seat,' he said slowly, 'please take my seat.'

She continued to ignore him. The bus driver was watching in his mirror. He half turned in his seat. 'Sit down, Limey,' he called impatiently over his shoulder, 'niggers ain't allowed to sit anywhere. Only on the back seat...'

O'Neill's neck and face turned scarlet. 'Sorry, miss,' he whispered, and he flopped back down on his seat.

Gordon was smiling broadly at his embarrassment. 'Serves you fucking right,' he whispered. 'It was perfectly obvious what you were after...'

The girl moved towards the front of the bus and three stops later she got off. O'Neill was quickly on his feet and followed behind her. He waved goodbye to Gordon's startled face through the window. The girl was mincing her way down the street, her bottom waggling provocatively with every step. O'Neill caught up with her and touched her elbow. She stopped and eyed him up and down.

'Yes?'

'I - I'm sorry about what happened on the bus,' O'Neill stammered. 'It was just that I didn't know about - about...'

'About how us niggers ain't allowed to sit on the whiteys' seats on our own buses?'

O'Neill could feel her anger but felt it was unfair that it should be directed at him. He nodded. 'Could - could we go somewhere and maybe have a drink and you could tell me....?'

'Where, man?' she interrupted him sharply. 'Which whitey bar will you bring me to? Which whitey bar do you think I can go into unless I'm the fucking barmaid?' She sucked in a long breath, her brown eyes hard with anger. 'Lookit, whitey, I know what you're after. Too goddam well I know what you're after, just like the rest of you whitey motherfucks.' She was jabbing her finger into his chest punctuating her words. 'You think that I ain't nothing but a black pussy that you can stick your goddam white cock up and then walk away and tell all your whitey pals that you fucking screwed yourself a bit of black American ham.' She smacked him hard across the face. 'So go fuck yourself, whitey.' She strode down the street leaving O'Neill in a state of shock, his hand to his cheek. He saw that passers-by were staring at him so he hurried into the nearest bar.

'A large whiskey, please,' he ordered from the black barman.

The barman shook his head, his gleaming teeth fixed in a set smile. 'Sorry sir,' he said. 'In Virginia state the sale of spirits is controlled and it ain't sold in bars. White folk are allowed buy one bottle per month in the Liquor Stores on production of a ration pass issued by the sheriff's office.' He smiled at O'Neill's astonishment. 'Beer only, sir, if you want to drink here. Ten cents a glass.'

O'Neill nodded. 'And have one yourself.' He handed the barman a dollar.

The barman shook his head. 'Thank you, sir,' he said, 'but coloured folk ain't allowed to drink in here...'

After three glasses of beer, O'Neill noticed the piano in the corner of the bar. He drained his glass and went over to it. A sudden thought struck him. He turned to the barman. 'In the state of Virginia,' he asked, 'is it permissible to hit the white keys as well as the black keys on this piano?'

The barman laughed. ' That there piano has been banged by so many drunken sailors down the years that blacks and whites is all the same. It's a bummer.'

O'Neill sat down on the stool and without thinking started playing Maria Elena. He was happy that the picture that leapt into his mind was that of Norma Perkins and not Madame Dupont. But the barman was right. The piano was so out of tune that he could hardly recognise what he was playing. He stopped in disgust and returned to the bar and ordered another drink. After his tenth glass he decided that he didn't really like ice-cold American beer, and he definitely didn't like Shit City. He caught the bus back to the dockyard.

Feeling the need to empty his bladder he stopped when he saw a lavatory block. There were two doors. One was marked 'Coloured men only' and the other was marked 'White men only'. He hiccoughed loudly as he debated the problem confronting him. Then he made up his mind.

'I don't feel like having a coloured man's piss and I don't want to have a white man's piss.' He looked around him to see if anybody was watching. 'So I'll have me a Jimmy O'Neill piss all on my own.'

Satisfied that he had made the right decision and that he was about to strike a blow for something or other that the black girl, if she were here, would approve of, he unbuttoned his flies and pissed a long satisfying piss up against the door of the white men's lavatory. Then he walked unsteadily to the Sudsbury's brow.

The quartermaster greeted him. 'Message for you Jack. The Pay Lieutenant said that if you came aboard before 21.00 hours you were to ring him in his cabin.'

O'Neill looked at his watch. It was only 20.30. Jesus, he thought, I've never been aboard so early in my life. He rang Lieutenant Davidson's cabin from the quartermaster's lobby.

'Ah, good,' Davidson said, immediately recognising O'Neill's voice. 'I'm sorry to impose on you at such short notice, old man, but do you think you could do just one more emergency modelling session for me. I promise it'll be the last...'

O'Neill quietly belched cold beer. 'Why not, sir?' he said cheerily. 'After all, yours is the best offer I've had all night...' And fuck Shit City, he thought.

Chapter Eleven

New York

New York was better. After five months in Norfolk it was O'Neill's turn to take the five days leave granted to the Care and Maintenance party, all that was left of Sudsbury's original crew. The rest had been returned to England on board a Royal Navy destroyer.

The destroyer had undergone refit in New York's dockyard and when she called to Norfolk, her supply assistant, sent ashore to pick up stores, asked O'Neill to post a letter which a member of the crew had written to his girlfriend in New York. O'Neill posted the letter that evening but first he made a note of the name and address. After all, he thought, if he's writing to her so soon, she's been tried and tested and not found wanting. And that might prove useful if ever he found himself at a loose end in New York.

He headed for the Big Apple with instructions from the Master-at-arms to report to the Services Club on Fifth Avenue where he would be provided with accommodation for the duration of his stay.

As far as O'Neill was concerned, the American hospitality offered by the Services Club made up for all the shortcomings of life in Shit City. The notice board inside the door asked invitingly, 'What will we do today?' And underneath were pinned a bewildering array of invitations. 'Mrs. Peloski invites three servicemen to dinner and afterwards to the show in Radio City. Apply at the desk.' 'A conducted tour of the Empire State Building and then on to lunch, followed by a tour of the Statue of Liberty. Five servicemen, please.' And so on. I'm going to enjoy this, O'Neill told himself.

When he checked in at the desk he was warmly welcomed and immediately transferred by taxi to a penthouse in Madison Avenue. His guide informed him that the elderly lady who owned it preferred to spend her winters in the comforting sunshine of Florida. Every Winter the penthouse, complete with butler and staff, was put at the disposal of the Services Club to accommodate five servicemen who were lucky enough to be placed there while on leave in New York. O'Neill could almost hear Hoskie congratulating him on the nice little place he had once again managed to find for himself

'This is really the only way to live,' he told himself, enjoying the luxury of the en suite bedroom to which James, the English butler, had escorted him.

'Breakfast is served in the dining room between eight and ten o'clock, sir,' James informed him. 'We do not serve luncheon but dinner is available at eight o'clock in the evening if you should desire it.' He drew down the covers on the double bed. 'It would be a great help, sir, if you could inform me before you go out in the mornings whether you will be returning for dinner.' O'Neill nodded. 'Oh, there is one other small matter, sir, which I hope you won't mind my mentioning.' James paused as he was about to close the door. 'I know that it will never arise, sir, but Mrs. Goodbody, our employer and your hostess, does insist that the guests do not bring back... er... other guests to the house at night, if you understand what I mean, sir.' He coughed discreetly behind his hand as if embarrassed to suggest that such a possibility could ever arise. 'If you need me at any time, just press the bell button...'

I will, I will, O'Neill thought happily, flopping onto the bed and bouncing up and down. He squeezed the roll of dollar bills in his pocket. He had taken £20 from one of the french letters and replaced it with an IOU. That, added to the £16 which Lieutenant Davidson paid him for modelling, amounted to over four months pay and guaranteed him a helluva week in New York. As he counted the dollars he vowed that from here in only the best was good enough for Jimmy O'Neill. Fate had obviously destined him for the good life!

After unpacking, he ambled down Madison Avenue to the Blue Room bar. It was Saturday night and the streets were crowded. Gordon, who had already been on leave to New York, had assured him that all a serviceman needed in any bar was the price of his first drink; after that, drinks would be bought for him by the other customers.

He ordered a glass of beer and sat at the bar. Sure enough, as soon as he drained the glass, a voice from the other end of the bar instructed the barman to 'set one up for the Limey'. O'Neill resented being called a Limey but decided that, in the interests of international co-operation, he would endure it for the period of his stay in America.

'Your good health, sir,' he called to the man who bought the drink. The man nodded back.

'Nothing's too good for you boys,' he said. 'Have a good time in New York.' O'Neill intended to do just that.

As he drank his beer - he had grown to like it cold - it occurred to him that the letter he'd posted in Norfolk had been to an address in Madison Avenue. He looked in his paybook and checked. Sure enough it was an apartment in 42nd and Madison Avenue, just two blocks from the Blue Room. Her name was Jo Rossini. And, furthermore, he found that she was in the telephone directory.

'Miss Rossini?' he asked when the telephone was answered. 'Miss Jo Rossini?' O'Neill felt wonderfully relaxed, fortified as he was with three beers and a large bourbon on the rocks. He was calling from the telephone lobby of the Blue Room.

'Yes, this is Jo Rossini.' There was a pause and O'Neill decided that he liked the husky voice at the other end of the line. It reminded him a little of Madame Dupont in Bermuda. And that must be good. 'Who is this? Who's calling?'

O'Neill took a deep breath. This was make or break time. 'My name's Jimmy O'Neill, Miss Rossini,' he said. 'I'm a sailor in the British Royal Navy and a few months ago I found a letter on the street in Norfolk, Virginia - obviously somebody lost it, and I posted it. I - I just wondered if you got it okay?'

There was another long pause. 'Why, yes, I did get the letter. I wondered why the envelope was so grubby.' O'Neill smiled to himself. That had been good thinking, rubbing it on the ground before he stuck it in the post-box. 'Thank you so much. It was from - from a friend...' Another pause. 'But where - where are you ringing from? I mean, you're not ringing from Norfolk, are you?'

O'Neill drained the bourbon. 'No, Miss Rossini.' He smiled. 'Actually, I'm just around the corner from you. In the Blue Room.' And then, as if the thought had just suddenly occurred to him: 'Would you care to join me? We could have a drink together....?'

Another long pause. 'Oh dear, oh dear, I'm sorry. I'm really sorry.' O'Neill frowned. It had looked good up to then. 'Sorry, what did you say your name was again?'

'O'Neill. Jimmy O'Neill.'

'Lookit, Jimmy, I really would like to meet you and - and thank you properly but there's this committee I'm secretary of and we have a meeting tonight and I just can't miss out on it. But what about breakfast in the morning? Could you come around to my apartment at about 9.30 and we'd have breakfast together and then we'd - we'd see....'

Indeed, we'd see! Jo Rossini turned out to be a bubbling Italian second-generation American, secretary to a bank manager and, O'Neill quickly deduced, well- heeled as all American women seemed to be. Her black hair fell in waves down to her shoulders, framing a beautiful oval face, wide generous mouth and sparkling teeth. O'Neill covertly cast an approving eye over the plump stretching curves flowing under her satin robe and decided that, once again, he had landed on his feet. And, what's more, she was in her mid thirties, an age group he was beginning to like more and more. Despite the accent, she reminded him more of Norma Perkins than Madame Dupont. He dismissed the thought quickly from his mind.

They had eaten breakfast. Jo looked at her watch. 'Oh, *mamma mia,*' she sighed, 'how time flies when you're in exciting company.' O'Neill had been telling her about the run to Malta. She stood up and pulled open the bow on the belt of her dressing gown. O'Neill's heart did a little skip. Then she tightened the robe about her and knotted the belt securely.

'You go and sit in the kitchen. Jimmy,' she smiled,' while I get - get myself ready.' She saw the laugh in his eyes and pushed him playfully out the door. He heard the lock click shut. 'Finish your coffee,' she called. 'I won't keep you waiting long. I have a little surprise for you.'

O'Neill glanced into the mirror and ran a comb through his hair. Things were looking up....

When she opened the door again she was fully dressed, a scarf on her head and a fur coat draped over her shoulders. She handed him his cap and overcoat. O'Neill put them on, a forced smile on his face. This was not what he expected.

'Ready?' she asked. He shrugged.

'If you are,' he said. 'Where - where are we going?' She chucked him playfully under the chin. 'I planned this little surprise for you last night just to welcome you to my home town.' She put on her coat. 'I'm going to take you on a mini-tour of New York. First we'll go to our local Art Gallery here on Madison - there's a wonderful collection of original Italian and Dutch paintings and some very fine American contemporaries that I just know you'll adore. Then we'll grab coffee and a sandwich somewhere and go on to visit the Statue of Liberty.' Her voice was bubbling with enthusiasm. 'Did you know that you can get right up inside the statue and look out through the jewels in her crown which are, in fact, windows?'

It wasn't the Statue of Liberty O'Neill had hoped he'd be crawling up that afternoon and doubts were beginning to form in his mind about this proposed mini-tour of New York. The Services Club arrangements for such outings struck him as being much better.

Jo looked at her watch. 'But we must hurry if we're going to catch the 11 o'clock Mass at St. Patrick's Cathedral first...' She noticed his startled grimace and looked at him in surprise. 'You are Roman Catholic, aren't you? Being Irish and all, I mean...I assumed....'

O'Neill nodded, trying to cloak his dismay. Suddenly, everything seemed to be going from bad to worse. They took a taxi to the Cathedral and Jo insisted on paying the fare. 'You're my guest in New York, Jimmy.' She beamed. 'And after what you've been through, nothing is too good for you boys...'

✛ ✛ ✛ ✛ ✛

He felt quite ashamed when he slipped out of the Cathedral while Jo was queuing for communion. He hailed a taxi and headed back down town. He wasn't Jo Rossini's type, he told himself, trying to allay his feelings of guilt, and, anyway, she's far better off keeping away from people like me. He took the piece of paper with her name and address on it out of his pay book.

You win some, you lose some, he thought. It must have been the fucking padre who wrote to her. He screwed the paper into a ball and pushed it down behind the cushion. He'd have to avoid the Blue Room for the duration of his stay in New York in case she came looking for him...

She didn't, but Paymaster Lieutenant Keith Davidson did. When O'Neill called to the Services Club to plan out his Monday, there was a message at the desk asking him to contact Lieutenant Davidson at the Hotel Aster on Fifth Avenue. He considered the situation and then decided he'd join a group of three to visit the Empire State Buildings with a Mrs. Japoski, and afterwards go on to lunch at her home in the Bronx. After that, if Mrs. Japoski hadn't made a better offer, he'd take in the Aster Hotel and see what Davidson wanted. And if it's anything to do with modelling, he thought, he can fuck off with himself.

If Mrs. Japoski made any offers, she didn't make them to O'Neill so he found himself that evening at the reception desk in the Aster asking for Lieutenant Davidson.

'Ah good, O'Neill, you got my message,' Davidson said when O'Neill phoned his room. 'I'm glad you happened to be in New York this week - a great bit of luck that!' O'Neill's brow furrowed. 'Wait for me in the bar and I'll join you in a few minutes. We have time for a drink before the show starts. I want you to meet a few people...'

'What - what show is this, sir?' O'Neill asked. Knowing the type Davidson was he didn't want to get walked into some highbrow thing that he wouldn't understand, especially when he could be at the vaudeville show he'd seen advertised down in a theatre on 87th street.

'The fashion show we spent so much time preparing for, of course.' Davidson said, surprised. 'It's on here in the hotel in about an hour and they've very kindly agreed to show my creations. Didn't they tell you at the Services Club?' O'Neill shook his head dumbly. If they had, he wouldn't be here. 'I'll meet you in the bar in ten minutes. Charge the drinks to my room...' O'Neill wondered if he made a run for it could he be found guilty of disobeying an order. He decided to wait.

He was glad he did. Davidson arrived with four of the most glamorous girls O'Neill had ever seen. His pulse quickened with pleasure. All four were tall and temptingly curved, all in the right places. The one with the red hair down around her shoulders, he decided, was the one for him, though either of the two blondes or the brunette would do equally well. He was on his feet before they arrived at the table.

'Evening sir,' he said. Davidson introduced him to his glamorous companions. 'Ladies, this is the Royal Navy's top fashion model, Jimmy O'Neill. Jimmy, meet Rusty, Jill, Betty and Justine.' He put his arm around O'Neill's shoulders. 'Without Jimmy's help I'd never have been able to have my collection ready for tonight.'

O'Neill felt himself reddening. 'Oh, look, how cute! He's blushing!' It was the redhead.

O'Neill blushed even deeper. Davidson came to his rescue. 'Go easy on him, Rusty,' he pleaded, 'he's new to the fashion world even though he's modelled the six garments you're showing tonight.'

Rusty took O'Neill's hand and squeezed it, her brown eyes deep pools of sex. 'So that's why I feel so - so excited when I'm wearing them.' She pushed her red hair back from her face, her lips pouting. 'I'd love to see you in action some time, sailor boy...and I don't mean on the ramp...' Her perfume was intoxicating. O'Neill was as hard as a rock.

Davidson looked at his watch. 'Okay, girls, backstage with you or Madame Fontaine'll have a fit. You're due on the ramp in twenty minutes...'

Rusty winked at O'Neill. 'Don't go without coming backstage, sweetheart,' she whispered, 'I want to hear all about the war - and things...'

All eyes watched them as the four flaunted themselves through the bar. Davidson beckoned to the waiter and sat down.

'You know something, Jimmy,' he said, his face thoughtful, 'everything's going so well for me, I can hardly believe my good luck.' He looked around the crowded bar. 'What you see here is the cream of New York society and tonight they're going to see the garments that you helped me create. Isn't that something?' He swallowed his drink at a gulp. 'I should feel great but when I think of that trip to Malta and all the poor bastards who were killed or maimed, and how well I'm doing out of it all, I don't feel that good...'

O'Neill's fingers closed on the fat roll of dollar notes in his pocket. He knew exactly how Davidson was feeling.

Davidson was right; his creations wowed the sophisticated New York fashion world. O'Neill was amazed when he saw Rusty hipping her way down the ramp in the garments he had worn in Davidson's cabin.

'Jesus, sir, did you redesign them, or what?' he asked incredulously. 'I mean, they didn't look like that on me, did they?'

Davidson nudged him in the ribs. 'It's Rusty's shape, old man,' he whispered, 'she's sort of more curvy than you....'

When they went backstage after the interval, O'Neill could hardly believe his eyes. Everything was organised chaos. Models coming off the ramp hurriedly stripped and were helped into the next creation. He had never before seen such a display of unconcerned nakedness. He watched Davidson adjusting one of the garments on a model. He was kneeling on the floor and lifted the skirt up around her naked thighs to smoothen down a seam. They were both totally unconcerned. I'll blow off if I stay here much longer, O'Neill thought.

Rusty came through the curtains from the ramp. She stood in front of him as the dresser helped her to slip off the organdie and tulle creation which had always made him half-hard when he modelled it. She was naked except for her skimpy briefs. Their eyes met. He tried to keep looking at her face. She pouted her lips, her tongue touching in and out.

'We're having a little party at Jill's place later, Jimmy,' she whispered, 'just Jill, Justine, Betty and myself.' She was already into another garment. 'Would you like to join us? It could be fun.'

O'Neill was feeling nicely tipsy when the five of them took the lift up to Jill's apartment. There was very little room in the lift and he found himself wedged firmly between Rusty and Justine, the intoxicating aroma of their bodies touching his nostrils and making him rigidly hard. Justine's hand brushed lightly against the bump in his trousers. She grinned and gave it a squeeze. He jerked away and bumped into Rusty. She looked down and saw his problem.

'Leave it be, Justine,' she whispered, her limpid eyes gazing into his, 'we're going to need all he's got before the night is out.'

Jill poured drinks for them in the apartment. She handed O'Neill a tumbler half full of bourbon. 'What games do you play in England?' she asked him.

O'Neill looked at her, puzzled. 'Games? You mean card games like poker or whist?' The four of them laughed.

No, darling,' Rusty told him, her eyes twinkling over the rim of her glass, 'when our Jill talks about games she has only one thing in mind and that's sex. She means sex games like, oh, Sioux Squaw Sex or Bronx Bouncers or such.'

O'Neill shook his head. 'Never heard of anything like that, I'm afraid,' he said. 'How - how do you play...?'

Jill drained her glass. 'Okay, everybody. Manhattan Mounts it has to be. The numbers are right - one cock and four pussies. This boy wants to know how to play....'

The four of them stood up and peeled off their clothes. They lined up before him naked. Three of them had stockings held up with black suspender belts but Rusty wore thigh-high red garters, each with an embroidered pink rosette. The colour of the garters exactly matched the shock of curly hair between her legs. O'Neill's eyes popped.

Jill and Rusty grabbed his hands and pulled him up out of the chair. 'Come on, sailor boy,' Jill told him, 'get those clothes off. You can't play all dressed up like that.'

O'Neill knew that he was blushing right down to his bulging penis. They stood watching in expectant silence as he took off his shirt and vest.

'Couldn't I do this in the bathroom?' he asked. Jill caught at his trousers and pulled it down around his ankles. Then she jerked down his underpants. His penis swung up erect.

'Oh my,' said Jill in admiration. 'Oh my!' Rusty reached out and slipped her hand under his manhood measuring the length along her wrist and forearm.

'Quite good for a Limey,' she said and squeezing him gently. Justine and Betty and Jill each had a feel and O'Neill didn't know where to look. He had never seen so much naked flesh before in his life.

'Okay then, sailor boy,' Jill ordered, 'get the rest of your clothes off and lie down on the rug. You have to measure us for jockey positions - whoever you say is the tightest gets the head, and the slackest gets the cockpit. The other two take right and left hand positions. Okay?'

O'Neill could feel the blood pounding through his body as he stretched out on the rug.

'But how do you mean....? He cut off in mid question when Jill squatted down and slipped his penis up inside her. She sat motionless for a few moments and then carefully lifted herself off. Rusty and Betty and Justine followed in quick succession. I must be dreaming, thought O'Neill. In fifteen seconds I've been up four of the most beautiful women in New York. This must be a dream.

'Right, sailor boy,' Jill said, 'decision time. Who is the tightest and who is the slackest?'

O'Neill had no idea. They were standing over him, teetering on their high heels, their long stockinged legs stretching invitingly open, their breasts hanging down as they awaited his decision. His penis, glistening, was swaying to the rhythm of his heart beats.

'Rusty's the tightest,' he said at last, 'and I think Jill might be the one a little on the slack side. But there's very little between them all.'

'Oh goody,' giggled Rusty, 'I get the head position, Jill's in the cockpit and Betty and Justine get a hand up each. So take up your riding positions, girls.' She squatted down, her knees on either side of O'Neill's head, the red shock of hair between her legs poised over his mouth. Jill was already on her knees astride him, his penis firmly tucked inside her. Betty and Justine knelt on either side of him and he felt his fingers being inserted.

'The rules of the race are simple, Jimmy,' Rusty told him. 'When I say go, you start kissing me.' O'Neill stared, fascinated. 'Betty and Justine work themselves off on your fingers, but Jill just sits still as she is now. Her job is to keep you on a hard as long as possible. Then when you make me come, I'll say, 'All change!' and we all swop around in a clockwise direction. Okay?' The curly red hair was tickling O'Neill's face. 'But what about me?' he asked, puzzled. 'What do I have to do?'

Rusty rubbed herself on his nose. 'Just waggle that tongue of yours.' She laughed. 'And any time you blow off, the jock on your cock has to get you hard again while the other three keep riding. You don't have to do a damned thing. We do all the work.' She looked back to see that the three were in position. Then she lowered herself onto O'Neill's waiting lips. 'Go!' she called.

O'Neill suddenly found himself being pounded by a pulsating pulchritude of female flesh. Except for Jill. She held him erect inside her while she waited impatiently for the three bobbing bottoms in front of her to stop. Rusty came almost immediately and in seconds they had swopped positions and were back in action again.

At such close quarters, Rusty was the only one O'Neill could recognise and she passed over him five times before Justine reported ruefully that, after his third blowout, she couldn't get O'Neill erect again. O'Neill gave Jill a last lingering kiss and then lay back exhausted on the rug.

'That's it,' said Justine regretfully, 'the game's over for the moment, I'm afraid.' She was holding his flaccid penis between her thumb and index finger. When she let go, it keeled over limply on his belly. 'See that, girls?' she asked. 'I'm afraid this poor boy's all fucked out...'

CHAPTER TWELVE

GIBRALTAR AND SICILY

Hoskins was in the first bed inside the door of Ward 20 in Portsmouth's Royal Naval Hospital. His eyes were closed, his face pinched and drawn. O'Neill was shocked to see how much his mate had faded since the run to Malta. He put his attache case under the bed and quietly pulled up a chair not sure whether he should wake Hoskie or let him sleep. He gave a little cough.

Hoskins's eyes fluttered open and his face lit up when he saw his visitor. 'Paddy!' He tried to pull himself to a sitting position. 'It's great to see you. I often wondered where you got to...' He saw the gold anchor on O'Neill's sleeve. 'And you got yourself promoted. Congratulations!'

O'Neill filled him in on how Chief Mullins had press-ganged him on to the Sudsbury. 'But how about you, Hoskie?' he asked. 'I thought you'd be out of hospital long ago. How's the ankle?'

Hoskins's lips puckered and he shook his head. 'It isn't,' he said ruefully. He pointed at the protecting cage that covered his legs. 'They - they had to cut the foot off...just above the ankle. It was smashed beyond repair, apparently.' He avoided O'Neill's shocked look.

'Oh Jesus, Hoskie, that's terrible, that's fucking terrible. I didn't know...' O'Neill saw tears gathering in Hoskins's eyes. 'I mean, couldn't they do anything...I mean....' His voice trailed off in frustrated embarrassment. He just didn't know what to say, what to do. They sat in silence. O'Neill wanted to reach out to Hoskins, to touch him but he couldn't bring himself to do it. He had never felt so inadequate in his whole life.

'I'm a married man now, you know,' Hoskins said at last. Then the words came tumbling out as if they had been locked up inside him. 'Pearl and I got married...they thought at first that the ankle would be alright and they left me out of here for a week and we got married in Liverpool. Then I had to come back and that's when they decided that my foot would have to come off. I've been here ever since though they tell me they'll be fitting an artificial leg in a week or two. Then I'll be discharged and I'll be as good as new...that's what they keep saying...'

The news that Pearl and Hoskie were married gave O'Neill the excuse he needed. He grasped Hoskie's hand in his, squeezed it and shook it vigorously in over-hearty congratulation. 'That's bloody great, Hoskie,' he grinned. 'You and Pearl getting married, I mean,' he added. 'I always knew that the two of you would make a go of it. How is she, by the way? And...and Mrs. Perkins. How are they?'

Hoskins sighed, his lips tightening. 'Pearl's pregnant,' he said quietly, avoiding O'Neill's eyes. 'The baby's due in three weeks or so. That's why we had to get married.' He sighed again. 'Mind you, Paddy, we'd have got married anyway - I mean, I do love Pearl. She's the best thing that ever happened to me, but...Jesus, I worry about the future, what with being a bloody cripple now, and with a wife and kid and having to live off Mrs. Perkins...' He forced a smile and met O'Neill's eyes. 'I'll tell you something for nothing, Paddy,' he whispered, 'don't ever trust a navy-issue french letter.' He shook his head wearily. 'I swear we only did it the once, Pearl and me, and that was the night before we left Liverpool for Bermuda and I used a french letter but it must have leaked or slipped or some fucking thing. The next I knew was when I got in touch with her after being brought here and she told me she was up the pole. Jesus, I couldn't believe it...'

O'Neill could feel his stomach tightening, a frightening thought beating inside his head. He tried to change the subject. 'What about her daddy, Tom Perkins, Butch... did he manage to get off the Pinewell...?'

Hoskins shook his head. 'No,' he said, 'he didn't. He was killed when a bomb went down the lift shaft. The whole marine crew of B Turret were killed in the explosion.' He turned to O'Neill. 'I never did thank you for getting me out. Only for you I'd have been a goner...' He reached out and took O'Neill's hand. 'Thanks, Paddy.'

O'Neill pulled his hand away, embarrassed. 'Fuck off, Hoskie. They couldn't kill a bad thing.' Another thought struck him. 'How many did get off her - I mean, the Chief and the other lads in the office and Godfrey..?'

Hoskins shook his head again. 'All gone,' he whispered, 'all fucking gone'

A shudder rippling through O'Neill as memory of the sinking of the Pinewell flooded his mind. 'All fucking gone? Jesus, we were lucky, bloody lucky...' He found himself thinking of Norma and forced himself to ask the question. 'How - how did Norma... Mrs. Perkins take it?' he asked, 'about Tom being killed, I mean.'

Hoskins held his gaze in a steady stare. 'It's hard to say,' he said at last. 'She doesn't talk about it much. You know he more or less left her but apparently he visited her at home the night before we sailed and they made it up.' Hoskins sighed again. 'They made it up too bloody well. Anyway, she's pregnant too - she's due about the same time as Pearl...' O'Neill dug into his pocket and took out his cigarettes, his fingers trembling so much he dropped the box of matches on the floor. He was thinking of what Tom Perkins told him that day they were sailing out of Liverpool harbour, how he had called on his wife the night before and she had slammed the door in his face...

Jesus, he thought, Norma and Pearl, both the same night. It couldn't be, could it? What have I done...? His foot hit against his attache case under the bed.

'Whatever you say about the navy's french letters,' he said, grasping hastily at the chance to change the subject, 'there was nothing wrong with the ones poor old Taffy Jones used....' He reached down and lifted the attache case on to the bed.

Hoskins watched him, perplexed. 'What french letters?' he asked. 'And what about Taffy? Did you meet him since? Did he get off alright...I never heard about him.'

O'Neill stopped, frowning.' But - but don't you remember, Hoskie? When we were on the raft? And we found poor Taffy and half his head blown off...' His voice trailed off as he realised that Hoskins didn't seem to remember how they had recovered the money in the french letters that Taffy wore as a lifebelt.

Hoskins shook his head, screwing up his face trying to recall what had happened. 'I'm totally blank about the whole thing, Paddy,' he said at last. 'I was drifting in and out of consciousness all night. I don't even remember being picked up...'

O'Neill paused and he fumbled hesitatingly at the lock of the attache case. Then he put it back down on the floor. If Hoskins couldn't remember about the money they recovered from Taffy's body... He sighed. You couldn't be that big a bollicks, could you? he asked himself.

Hoskins was waiting. 'What about Taffy, Paddy,' he asked again.

O'Neill's eyes met his. 'I'll tell you what about Taffy,' he whispered at last, looking around to make sure the patients in the other beds couldn't hear. And he quickly went back over the events leading up to the finding of Taffy's body. 'You must remember, Hoskie, for God's sake,' he insisted, 'it was you knew that Taffy had the money in the french letters...'

Hoskins was nodding. 'Yeah, I knew Taffy always carried the canteen takings on him when we were at sea,' he said . 'He told me so one night we were both fairly pissed in the Green Man but I still don't remember...'

O'Neill put the attache case on the bed and opened it an inch or two so that Hoskins could see the contents.

Hoskins breath whistled out of him. 'Jesus, Paddy!' He reached out and fingered the notes as if to check they were real. 'There must be hundreds there...'

'Not hundreds, Hoskie,' O'Neill said quietly. 'Thousands! To be exact, four thousand five hundred and sixty quid, less the twenty I blew in New York, and every fucking penny of it belongs to you and me.' He snapped the case shut and put it back under the bed. Hoskins was lying back on the pillow, flabbergasted.

'I brought it in today to let you see it, Hoskie,' O'Neill whispered, 'but first thing tomorrow I'll put it in the bank here in Pompey - half in your name and half in mine. Okay ? Straight down the middle.' He patted Hoskie's shoulder encouragingly. 'So you see, things aren't as bad as you thought. With a pension and that sort of money, you and Pearl should be reasonably comfortable.'

O'Neill looked around when the ward door opening behind him. Pearl, her stomach bulging with her baby, was standing in the door. When she saw O'Neill, the colour flooded into her face.

He stood up and held out his hand. 'Pearl! Great to see you again and congratulations,' he blustered to hide his own confusion. 'Hoskie's been telling me all the news.'

Pearl recovered her composure and demurely presented her cheek for a kiss. She squeezed his hand. 'Good to see you too, Paddy,' she said. 'You're looking great - as handsome as ever...' Her cheek was pressed against his and over her shoulder he saw her mother standing in the doorway. His heart gave a little skip.

Norma Perkins went to back out again, then hesitated and pulled her coat closed in front of her as if trying to hide the fact that she was pregnant. They looked at one another for long moments. Norma's dark hair tumbled around her face, her eyes filled with embarrassment.

Jesus, thought O'Neill, you are beautiful and I love you more than ever. He released Pearl and faced Norma. 'Hello.. ah.. Mrs. Perkins,' he said at last. He held out his hand and she took it in hers.

'Hello, Jimmy,' she said. 'Nice to see you again.' She was studying his face. 'You haven't changed since... since...' They both blushed, remembering the last time, the night in his bedroom in Liverpool. She looked past him at Hoskins in the bed. 'What do you think of our patient? Your visit seems to have cheered him up considerably. He's looking much more lively than the last time we were down.' She turned back to O'Neill. 'And he told us how you saved his life...'

O'Neill's lips twitched. 'Ah, don't mind Hoskie....' he started and suddenly remembered Tom Perkins. He groped for words. 'I just heard about Butch... about Mr. Perkins. I -I'm sorry...'

Norma's hands fluttered involuntarily down to her bulging tummy. 'It was... ah... a terrible shock when I got the notification of his death,' she whispered. 'So many people killed in just a few minutes... and not knowing about George and yourself... but let's not talk about it. How I wish this horrible war was over. And I just hope and pray that you'll never have to go back to that terrible Mediterranean place again...'

Norma's hopes and prayers came to nothing. Barely a month later O'Neill was sitting in a bar in Gibraltar sipping at a glass of rum and coke. Two days after his hospital visit to Hoskins, HMS Sudsbury was ordered back to the Mediterranean. There she joined the battleship Warspite and the aircraft carrier Indomitable. The carrier had spent nearly nine months in Liverpool undergoing repairs after the Malta convoy. The strongest buzz said that the squadron was there to cover an imminent invasion of Greece.

O'Neill was thinking of Norma and Pearl. Their babies would be born now. Jesus, here he was, a daddy to two kids and he didn't want to know about it. He sighed and drained his drink. What a horrible mess his first time on the job had made of all their lives. Anyhow, he had done all he could to shoulder his share of the responsibility. When he paid the money into the bank in Pompey he put three thousand, five hundred and forty pounds in the account he opened up for Hoskins and the other thousand in his own account. That should leave Hoskins fairly comfortable.

'Jimmy O'Neill! I don't fucking believe it!' O'Neill looked up in surprise at the excited shout. 'It is Jimmy O'Neill, isn't it?' A soldier was standing at the bar, a pint of beer in his hand, his face browned from the sun. O'Neill recognised him immediately - Jack Hayes, a near neighbour in the village in Co. Meath. About five years ago they sat beside one another in school and then the Hayes family moved to England and he hadn't seen or even thought about him since.

'Jack! Jack Hayes!' O'Neill said disbelievingly, 'a shagging squaddie, and a sergeant, no less.' He examined the flash on Jack's shoulder which proclaimed that Hayes was a soldier of the 1st Airborne Division of the 8th Army. 'Does that mean that you go jumping out of aeroplanes?' he asked, 'I always knew you had a screw loose in that head of yours..' He ordered a round of drinks.

Jack Hayes was still pumping his hand. 'I tell you something for nothing, mate,' he laughed. 'I'd rather jump out of an aeroplane any day than go on one of them ships of yours. Jesus, the thought of being trapped in one of those and water everywhere...' He shook his head dolefully. 'I came out here on a troopship and I never slept a wink because of the thought of drowning. I hate bloody water. Give me the desert every time.' He gulped down the last of his pint. 'But tell me all about yourself, Jimmy. And what does that gold anchor thing on your arm mean..?'

After three more drinks, O'Neill felt in the mood for some action. He looked around the bar. Apart from the plump senorita in flowing skirts banging out a bored fandango on the platform stage in the corner of the bar, there were only sailors and soldiers and not a girl in sight.

'Where the hell are all the women in Gibraltar?' he asked, mystified. 'They must be some somewhere.'

Hayes laughed. 'When the fleet's in, their daddies keep them locked up in case you randy shaggers get at 'em.' He drained his drink. 'This kip's dead. I know a better place down by the Alemeda Gardens - there'll be some action there. Drink up and we'll chance our luck..'

While Leading Supply Assistant O'Neill and Sergeant Hayes were plotting a combined action on the women of Gibraltar, others, of more senior rank, were planning Operation Husky - the assault on Sicily which Churchill had called the 'soft underbelly of Europe'.

General Eisenhower had moved his headquarters to Algiers and with General Patton in command of the American 7th Army and General Montgomery in command of the British 8th Army, the Combined Chiefs of Staff were finalising the details of Operation Husky.

The assault forces were to be assembled from the United States, Britain, North Africa and Egypt and 3,000 aircraft and 3,200 ships would be required to transport them. Convoys would have to escorted across wide oceans and ferried through narrow channels so that 160,000 men, 14,000 vehicles, 600 tanks and 1,800 guns would all arrive off the south-east coast of Sicily on the night of July 10th. Airborne troops and paratroops would be landed from American planes towing flimsy plywood gliders each carrying dozens of troops and their supplies. All this to be carried out hopefully undetected by enemy forces.

The plans of O'Neill and Hayes, less complicated than Eisenhower's but demanding equal dedication, had gone quite well. The Alemeda Bar, just opposite the Garden Park, was crowded but they found a vacant table. They were joined by two girls. After a few drinks and a chat-up in gesticulating pidgin English and Spanish, O'Neill opted for a walk in the Gardens with Carla, the taller of the two.

'It ees nice a time for walk, yes?' The darkness was closing in fast and the Alemeda Gardens were alive with birdsong and the cloying perfume of the exotic shrubbery. Carla was clinging to O'Neill, his arm around her slim waist. Her brown eyes were alive with promise and she giggled when O'Neill led her off the path and into the bushes. She flopped down on the grass when they found a clearing and O'Neill stretched down beside her. Her body clung to his, her arms around his neck. He could feel her hard breasts jutting against him.

'I give you good time,' she whispered, her full lips bruising his, her tongue touching in and out of his mouth.

O'Neill's hand slid down to her thigh. She squeezed more tightly against him. He slid his hand up her leg under the skirt and fondled the bare skin above her stocking. Her fingers were caressing the bump in his trousers, fumbling to unbutton his flies. She strained as his hand closed between her legs. She had no knickers on.

'Jesus!' O'Neill exclaimed. He sat up in disbelief looking down at Carla's face.

Her eyes were suddenly anxious. 'I give you good time... ' she repeated in a whisper, tightening her arms around O'Neill. He pushed himself to his feet, struggling as Carla tried to restrain him. O'Neill pushed her roughly from him and strode back down through the Gardens to the Alemeda Bar, a shrill tirade of Spanish abuse following him on the night air.

'I don't fucking believe this,' he whispered, a grin coming over his face as he began to appreciate the funny side of the situation. He looked down at the hand which had touched Carla's private parts and rubbed it on the side of his jacket as if to clean it. Hayes was still at the table with the other girl.

'That was a quick one, Jimmy, even for short time,' He grinned over the rim of his glass. 'Was he any good?'

O'Neill's eyes widened. 'Was he any good?' he repeated in surprise. 'You mean you knew all the time...?'

Hayes looked puzzled. 'Knew what?' he asked.

'That - that he wasn't a girl,' O'Neill stuttered. 'I mean that the shagger I went with was a bloody man...'

Jack Hayes laughed till the tears ran down his cheeks. He wiped at his eyes with the sleeve of his jacket. The girl with him joined in heartily though she didn't understand a word they were saying. Hayes drained his glass and, leaning forward, he lifted the girl's skirts so that O'Neill could see what was between her legs. She wasn't wearing knickers either. O'Neill's eyes popped.

'They're all fucking men, Jimmy boy,' Hayes told him. 'Didn't you know that? This is where they hang out - in the Alemeda Gardens. And those that don't dress up as women wear a white rose behind their ears so that you'll know exactly what they're offering.' He shook his head in disbelief. 'Don't you blokes in the Navy get told any fucking thing?'

July 10 was to be the day of assault on Sicily. For fully a week before, intense air attacks had been made, day and night, on the airfields both there and in Sardinia. On the morning of July 9, from the south and the east and the west, great convoys of ships of all sizes and shapes loomed out of the rising mists, all converging south of Malta. That afternoon the order was given to steam for the beaches of Sicily .

O'Neill and Chief Mullins stood at the f'xle rail watching out as the carrier, Indomitable, steamed a cable length away on their port quarter. Chief Mullins shook his head gloomily as aircraft landing on the carrier's flight-deck.

'Just our fucking luck to get landed with that cow,' Mullins grunted, dragging on his cigarette. 'She's bad luck, that one.' He tossed the butt of the cigarette over the side. 'Did you know that?' O'Neill shook his head. 'I got her whole history from a stoker I had a few drinks with back in Gib,' the Chief told him. 'She was built in Barrow in Furness in 1941 and went straight out to the West Indies for working-up trials and ran on a coral reef going into Kingston harbour.' Mullins shook his head at the crass stupidity of naval officers in general. But knowing from bitter experience the type of half-wits who were made officers, like the fucking dressmaker they themselves had for a Paybob, nothing really surprised him any more.

'There she was, after costing millions of pounds, due to go on to Cape Town to provide air cover for the battle wagons, Prince of Wales and Repulse, but in the middle of the fucking afternoon, in Kingston harbour, in bloody broad daylight, she piles up onto a coral reef, could you believe it?'

According to the stoker, that meant that the two battleships had to travel to the East Indies without air-cover and the Japs sunk both of them.

'From there on,' said Mullins, 'it's been all down hill for Indomitable. Look what happened at Malta. She got herself blown out of the water. I was watching when it happened - she lost 130 killed in a few seconds when she was dive-bombed.' He shook his head dolefully. 'That fucking carrier has been responsible for sinking more British ships and killing more unfortunate British matelots than a whole squadron of Jerry submarines. She's bad luck, is that one...'

As Indomitable took up station again after flying off aircraft, O'Neill saw the vast convoys of landing craft, all packed with American soldiers, plunging northward from Malta and the African ports between Bizerta and Benghazi. Through his binoculars he could see the ungainly craft heaving in the heavy swell. Most of the soldiers seemed to be seasick and were vomiting uncontrollably. He'd been seasick himself for nearly three months when he first joined Manway. He knew exactly how they felt.

'God help them,' he said to Chief Mullins, 'the last thing those poor bastards need is to have to fight when they hit the beaches.'

Overhead they heard the drone of hundreds of aircraft, many with gliders in tow, heading north into the gathering dusk. O'Neill thought of Sergeant Hayes and their night out in Gibraltar. Better you up there than me, Jack, he thought. Good luck!

Sergeant Hayes and his platoon were huddled in a light plywood glider being towed by an American Dakota. Every man had over 70 pounds of armament and equipment strapped to his back making it difficult to relax in the narrow cramped seats. The noise from the engines of the hundreds of towing planes made it almost impossible to carry out a conversation but Hayes noted that his platoon were nervous and didn't have too much to say anyway. He wasn't worried. They were good men, well trained, and they all knew from experience that when the time came they could depend on one another.

The green light over the cockpit door started flashing in the dark of the cabin. Sergeant Hayes lips tightened. He felt the sudden rise in tension. The silence in the glider after the towing craft had slipped it was electrifying. This was it, they were on their way down.

'Stand by, lads,' he called, 'brace yourselves for landing.'

The glider hit heavily and bounced up into the air. Then it bounced again and the thin plywood shell of the craft disintegrated, scattering the soldiers in a disorganised pile. Water burst in through the fractured sides and enveloped them in a green frothy spume.

'Jesus,' a terrified voice screamed, 'the stupid bastards have dropped us short. We're in the fucking sea.'

Sergeant Hayes realised that the screaming voice was his own. The waters of the Mediterranean closed over him. Weighed down by 70 pounds of equipment, he and his whole platoon were drowned in seconds. They didn't even see the thousands of their companions, also dropped short of the beaches, who drowned beside them. Operation Husky had got off to a bad start.

Much to Chief Mullins's surprise the beachhead in Sicily had been secured by July 12th and both the British 8th Army and the American 7th Army were advancing steadily. The tannoy on Sudsbury came alive.

'Captain speaking. I want to confirm that the assault on Sicily has been satisfactorily mounted and is proceeding according to plan. The squadron has now been ordered to take up position off Tarranto harbour where heavy units of the Italian fleet are anchored. Our task will be to engage and destroy them should they venture out on the open sea. That is all.'

'That is all,' groaned Chief Mullins to O'Neill in the Victualling Office. 'Heavy units! That means bloody battleships and they'll blast us out of the water before we'll even get within range. I knew everything was going too smoothly...'

Two days went by and all was quiet. The atmosphere on the ship was now one of euphoric expectation. The buzz was that the squadron would shortly be returning to Malta.

Deciding that the night was too warm for sleeping in the mess, O'Neill set up his camp-bed on the port well-deck and made ready to kip down for the night. He was looking forward to Malta - he'd heard wonderful accounts of life on the island now that the long siege was successfully lifted.

The tannoy rattled. 'D'ye hear there. Indomitable will be carrying out night flying exercises, starting at 22.00 hours.'

Sudsbury heeled as she veered off at 20 degrees to keep station. O'Neill sighed. He'd better get his head down quickly or he'd get no kip with Indomitable's aircraft thundering around in circles, flying off and landing on.

He was still awake an hour later, staring wide-eyed at the clouded sky when a plane roared by just a few feet above sea-level. For a frightening second or two he saw Italian markings on the wings. He was out of the camp-bed and pulling on his shorts when the explosion lit up the face of the sea on the port beam. He watched in awe as a huge pillar of water towered high above Indomitable's flight-deck and she veered drunkenly off to starboard. Sudsbury's siren hooted and the alarm bells for Action Stations sounded through the ship.

O'Neill was hurrying to his action station at the Cipher Office when he met a dishevelled Chief Mullins.

'What the fuck's going on?' the Chief demanded. 'Is it that fucking carrier again?'

O'Neill nodded. 'An Italian bomber joined in the exercise with the carrier's planes and got her straight in the guts with a torpedo.' The Chief shook his head despairingly now fully convinced that all British naval officers were imbeciles.

'Here we are in the middle of a fucking invasion of Italy and that stupid carrier has to have night flying exercises..' He shook his head. 'I knew she was bad luck. I told you...'

In a broadcast to the world, Prime Minister Churchill said that the Sicilian campaign was now successfully concluded and everything had gone exactly according to plan.

Supply Chief Petty Officer Mullins offered no comment. He got out the rum jar and poured out two measures for himself and O'Neill. 'Hopefully, we'll never see that fucking Indomitable cow again,' he toasted.

'I'll drink to that, Chief,' said O'Neill and they drained their glasses. And I'll write a letter to Norma soon, he thought. Just as soon as we get to Malta...

CHAPTER THIRTEEN

NORMANDY

On June 6, 1944, after nine months bombarding the coast of Italy, HMS Sudsbury's red-hot guns now poured salvo after salvo over the Omaha beachhead in Normandy. Operation Overlord, the long-awaited assault on Europe, had been ordered by General Eisenhower.

The Captain, in his tannoy address, described the operation as 'a bloody beginning to a glorious end.' O'Neill hoped he knew what he was talking about.

The Allied supremacy on the sea and in the air was firmly established. Sudsbury's crew was left under no doubt that they were taking part in the greatest invasion in the history of the world. The Captain, had read Eisenhower's 'Address to the Soldiers, Sailors and Airmen of the Allied Expeditionary Force' in which he emphasised that their task would not be an easy one.

'Your enemy is well trained, well equipped and battle-hardened,' he told them. 'He will fight savagely... but I have full confidence in your courage, devotion to duty and skill in battle. We will accept nothing less than a full victory.'

Sudsbury closed up at action stations at 04.30 and moved slowly down the swept channel towards their allotted bombardment position continually under helm as they dodged the hundreds of small craft carrying the soldiers to the beach. At 05.30 the bombardment of the coastline opened up right along the wide front. At 08.30 after three hours of intense bombardment, with little or no return fire from the German shore batteries in their sector, Sudsbury reverted from action stations to defence stations.

It was still only 0900 hours but Chief Mullins poured out a tot of rum for O'Neill and himself in the Victualling Office.

'Wouldn't you think they'd give us a few days leave before throwing us in at the deep end again?' grunted the Chief before swallowing back his drink. 'Anyhow, I hope this Eisenhower man knows what he's on about this time round. We heard enough of his glory-boy Yankee shit before Sicily and that was bloody near a God-almighty cock-up as we too fucking well know. And why should we think this lot will be any different?'

After stand-easy tea, O'Neill slipped out of the Victualling Office and went up on deck to watch history being made. High above him the continuous roar of bombers pouring across the sky left a deadening pall of noise that added to the sickening din of war on the sea. The rumble and flare of exploding bombs transformed the distant shoreline into an eerie canvas of dark and light.

Everywhere, as far as the eye could see, were ships of all shapes and sizes. Hundreds of landing craft bobbed in a monotonous stream of deadly purpose towards the beach. Each was packed with tense soldiers, some veterans of previous campaigns, most mere boys hearing for the first time the angry scream of war. LSTs, laden with heavy tanks, wallowed their way towards the distant beaches, trying to hold course in the heavy swell. O'Neill watched, fascinated. No way, he decided, could he ever be a soldier.

The tannoy rattled 'Up spirits.' It was comforting to know that, invasion or no invasion, life in His Majesty's navy would go on as usual.

Three days later, with the beachhead safely secured, HMS Sudsbury was ordered to steam westward towards Cherbourg. Hour after hour they bombarded targets selected for them by a RAF spotter aircraft flying between them and the shoreline. The Gunnery Officer was in radio contact with the plane's pilot who kept him informed of the success or otherwise of his efforts. O'Neill watched through binoculars.

The pilot gave the bearing of a well-camouflaged shore battery he'd spotted in a wood east of Cherbourg. He invited Sudsbury's Gunnery Officer to 'fire for effect'. This would enable him to see where the shells were landing and if necessary give correcting bearings.

O'Neill's ear-drums popped at the roar of Sudsbury's guns and he focused his binoculars on the distant plane. Suddenly it veered violently and broke into two parts. He lowered his binoculars in disbelief. Jesus, he realised, a shell from Sudsbury's forward turret has actually sliced the fucking thing in two. He refocused his binoculars and watched as the two halves of the plane spiralled slowly down and splashed into the grey waters of the Channel.

Sudsbury's Gunnery Officer waited impatiently for his spotter to report how the shoot had gone. The radio remained silent despite his repeated impatient calls. 'Fucking brylcreem boys,' he grumbled at the Gunner's Mate, 'they're never in the place where you want them to be.'

O'Neill said nothing. He was thinking of Jack Hayes and Sicily. When he returned to the office. Chief Mullins told him that Paymaster Lieutenant Baysworth wanted to see him in his cabin. Baysworth, a regular navy officer had replaced Lieutenant Davidson as Sudsbury's Supply Officer.

'I'd say it's about your examination for promotion to petty officer,' the Chief told him. 'He was asking me about you and I gave you a good reference.' He grinned at O'Neill's worried expression. When O'Neill requested to do the exam a few weeks before, Lieutenant Davidson was still on board and O'Neill felt a lot more confident then than he did now.

Lieutenant Baysworth was in expansive mood. He had O'Neill's records open in front of him on the desk. 'Sit down, O'Neill,' he said, pointing to the chair beside him. ' I've been reading what Lieutenant Davidson said about you - found you indispensable, it says here. In fact, he told me that himself before he left.'

O'Neill suppressed a smile. He knew exactly what Davidson was thinking about when he wrote that, and it had a lot more to do with his performance on the ramp than in the Victualling Office.

'Chief Mullins also regards you highly and says you know your job from A to Z.' Baysworth closed the file. 'So why should I waste my time, your time and everybody's time asking you stupid questions? I'd have to look up the answers in the Manual and I've no doubt you know them already.' He held out his hand. 'The Chief says you'll make an excellent petty officer and that's good enough for me. Congratulations. As from now, you're Supply Petty Officer O'Neill...'

'Well, what did the Paybob have to say for himself?' Chief Mullins asked when O'Neill returned to the office. He had a cup of grog in his hand.

O'Neill grinned. 'There was good news and bad news, Chief,' he said. 'Which do you want first?'

The Chief sipped at the grog, his eyes narrowing. 'Let's have it all together, son,' he said. 'That way I can handle it better.'

O'Neill nodded, filling himself out some grog from the sink. 'The good news, Chief, is that, thanks to your good self and Lieutenant Davidson, I don't have to do the exam - I'm being promoted to petty officer right away.' He paused for effect. 'The bad news is that he wants to stock-take tomorrow...'

Chief Mullins spluttered into the cup, splashing grog down the front of his jacket. O'Neill had to slap him repeatedly on the back to relieve the fit of choking that shook him. There were tears in the Chief's eyes when he finally subsided into the chair. He shook his head, once again overcome at the utter stupidity of his so-called superiors.

'Didn't he hear fucking Eisenhower saying that we had embarked on a glorious mission to free the oppressed people of Europe?' Mullins demanded. 'Right now the greatest invasion the world has ever seen is taking place out there. Any minute we could come under fire from Nazi shore batteries in Cherbourg and be blown out of the sea and you tell me that half-wit wants to go counting fucking bags of sugar in Number 2 store...'

'Well, he didn't exactly specify that it was the bags of sugar in No. 2 Store that he wanted to count...'

O'Neill and Shorty Smith spent the afternoon doing a trial stock-take of the provisions in Numbers 1 and 2 Stores and finally agreed that everything tallied with the ledger figures except for the sugar. According to the Ledger there should be twelve bags of sugar in No. 1 Store and ten in No. 2 Store. However, despite checking and cross-checking, though there were twelve bags in No. 1 Store there were only five in No. 2 Store.

'The Chief must have done another one of his little deals in Pompey,' Smith grinned. 'You notice, he knew immediately that 'twas the sugar in No. 2 Store that was short.'

An alarming thought struck O'Neill. 'Jesus, I hope he's not up there praying for another fucking bomb,' he said. 'Let's get the hell out of here!'

When O'Neill handed over the results of their stock-take, the Chief nodded thoughtfully and rolled himself a cigarette. 'Can't understand this,' he said, 'can't understand this at all'. He turned to Smith. 'You were on duty the evening we took on stores in Pompey?' Smith nodded dumbly. 'You stupid little bollocks! I told you to check everything carefully. How did you let them pinch five bags of sugar from under your nose?' He waved Smith's protests aside. 'Fuck off out of here and let me think this one out.'

Smith left hurriedly, glad to escape the Chief's wrath even though he knew he was the innocent party.

The Chief eyed O'Neill, his lips pursed. 'Congratulations on your promotion,' he said, at last. 'I've brought you from Supply Assistant to Supply Petty Officer in two years without even doing a bloody exam. That's some achievement, believe me.' His eyebrows lifted. 'Now then, about these five bags of sugar. D'you think you could handle that little matter for me, now that you're practically a Chief Pusser yourself?' He had the rum jar out.

O'Neill nodded, smiling. 'No problem, Chief,' he said, washing out two cups in the sink.

Next day Lieutenant Baysworth, Chief Mullins and Tanky spent the forenoon watch taking stock in No. 1 Store and then adjourned for dinner. O'Neill and Smith spent their dinner hour humping five bags of sugar from No. 1 Store to No. 2 Store.

'How did it go, Chief?' O'Neill asked when the Chief and Tanky returned to the Victualling Office, the stock-take completed.

The Chief nodded, flopping into his chair. 'Help yourself to a tot, Tanky,' he invited, 'you earned it.' He turned to O'Neill, smiling. 'No problems,' he said, 'everything bang on.' He saw Smith smirking. 'And if you ever let that happen to me again, you gormless sprog, I'll have your guts for fucking garters...'

A week later, HMS Sudsbury tied up at the wall in Portsmouth dockyard. Supply Petty Officer O'Neill shook Chief Mullins's hand at the brow. A shapely Wren, driving a naval van, was waiting to transport him and his kit to the naval barracks. Smith had humped O'Neill's kit-bag and hammock over the brow to the van and was chatting-up the Wren.

'I'm two years over-due that shore job you talked me out of after the run to Malta,' O'Neill said. 'I hope I get it now. I've had a gut-full of the sea and I wouldn't mind spending the rest of the war on dry land.'

Chief Mullins nodded in agreement. 'A word of advice to you, son, from an old pusser who's been through the good and the bad.' His voice dropped to a whisper so that the quartermaster wouldn't hear. 'Remember always to look after number one in this man's navy. This war'll be over soon and we could all be back on the scrap-heap selling matches again like the last time. So look after yourself while you can. Nobody else cares a shit about you.' He shook O'Neill's hand heartily. O'Neill came to attention and saluted.

'You know something,' Chief Mullins said, returning the salute, 'I do believe I'll miss you, you Irish bollocks. And don't ever forget what I told you - look after number one...'

O'Neill spent two weeks leave in Ireland. He was looking forward impatiently to getting back to Liverpool to call on Norma. He had a quick drink in the Green Man to bolster his courage. It felt strange walking down the old familiar streets where he had lived for nearly three months when he first joined the ill-fated Pinewell. His heart was thumping when he knocked on the door of Norma Perkins's house.

'Hello Norma,' he said nervously when she opened the door.

'Jimmy! Jimmy O'Neill!' Norma brushed the hair back from her face. Her eyes lit up in welcome, no sign whatsoever of the embarrassment she had shown when they last met in the hospital when she was eight months pregnant. O'Neill thought he had never seen her look so beautiful. 'And my goodness me, you've been promoted again! Come on in and let me see you.'

O'Neill felt himself blushing and cursed himself for it. How come she always manages to make me blush, he wondered. Norma walked around him admiring the new uniform with the brass buttons and the crown and crossed anchors with one good conduct stripe on the arm.

'You know something. Jimmy O'Neill,' she said slowly, 'I do believe that the promotion has matured you.' She searched for the right words. 'You look more - more responsible, somehow.' She reached up and kissed him lightly on the tip of his nose. His arms closed around her but she slipped through them and pushed him away.

'It -it's great to see you, Norma,' he said.' I think of you all the time, you know – you and Pearl and Hoskie.'

'But not often enough to sit down and write us a letter?' she accused. 'Don't you realise how much I - how much we worry about you not knowing where you are or even whether you're alive or dead. Twice you've written in two years.'

O'Neill nodded, embarrassed again. 'I'm sorry, Norma,' he said. 'I've started so many letters to you but I never manage to get them finished. It's because I know they're going to be read by some stupid censoring officer before you get them. And I want our... I want us..' His voice trailed off. 'How - how's Hoskie, by the way?' he asked lamely. 'Did he ever manage to get a job or what's he at?'

Norma was filling the kettle to make tea. She turned to him in surprise. 'Didn't you get his letter?' she asked. 'He wrote and told you all about the shop, about how he bought a shop. You remember the newsagents and sweet shop just around the corner? That's the one. The man who owned it, he was in the army and he was killed and his wife went back to Glasgow to her mother. George bought the shop. He and Pearl run it now and they're doing ever so well. Oh, they're so grateful to you. You were so good to George...'

She stopped when a high-pitched wail came from upstairs. Her face reddened. 'Oh dear,' she said at last, 'one of the children is awake. They were having their nap. I was hoping...'

O'Neill took the kettle from her. This was the moment he had dreaded. 'How - how old are they now?' he asked. He put the kettle back on the stove.

Norma hesitated, avoiding his eyes. 'They're nearly a year and a half now,' she said. 'They were born within two days of each other.' The crying stopped. She listened, obviously relieved.

'I - I'd love to see them,' O'Neill said at last. 'May I?' Norma hesitated and then shrugged. He followed her up the stairs. Norma opened the door quietly. This used to be his room. This was where...

There were two cots. He looked down into the first one and felt his face going red. The little boy's face, the mouth puckered with dimpled cheeks was his own. The resemblance was uncanny. Jesus, he thought, the whole world must be able to see that.

Norma fussed over the other cot. 'This is George's little girl,' she whispered. 'They called her Norma after me. Wasn't that nice of them?'

O'Neill looked down at the sleeping child. 'She's the spitting image of Pearl,' he whispered, relieved. 'She's beautiful.' He looked back at the other cot. 'What - what did you call the little boy?'

Norma's eyes met his at last. 'I called him after his daddy,' she said. O'Neill's heart missed a beat. 'Tom. Tom Perkins.' She bent down and touched the baby's cheek. 'He's the most beautiful boy in the whole world and I'm so glad I had him. He means everything to me...'

She turned suddenly and reached up to put her arms around O'Neill's neck. He pulled her to him, feeling himself hardening. Their lips met in a long kiss.

'Do you remember the night you took me out and played the piano and sang to me in the YMCA?' she whispered.

O'Neill nodded. 'Maria Elena, you're the answer to a prayer...' he sang softly. He kissed her again. 'A love like our is great enough for two...' Then he added: 'And the air-raid shelter and - and later... d'ye think I could ever forget?'

Norma pushed him away, holding him at arm's length, her eyes moist. She smiled. 'Maria Elena will always be our song,' she whispered. 'I even bought the record and I play it all the time on the gramophone. You know something, Jimmy O'Neill, you were the best thing that ever happened to me. Don't ever feel guilty about - about anything. There's no regrets on my side and there need be none on yours.' His arms closed around her and they kissed passionately.

Norma looked around, smiling. 'I always think this is the nicest room in the house. It has - it has such wonderful memories for me.' She squeezed his hand. 'Now let's go and have that cup of tea. Then you can go around and see George and Pearl. They'll love to see you.'

He followed her out of the room with a backward glance at the two cots. Half way down the stairs he stopped. 'Just want to go to the bathroom,' he said.

'You know where it is,' Norma answered.

O'Neill crept back into the bedroom and stood over the cots looking down from one tiny, sleeping face to the other. He touched their foreheads gently. 'I'll be back to be your real dad some day when this damn war is over' he whispered to his son. 'And I'll be the best uncle you'll ever have' he told little Norma, He touched their foreheads again. 'I hope so, anyhow.' He felt his eyes going moist and brushed at them angrily. 'Bye, ah.. Tom. Bye Norma.' Then he followed Norma down the stairs.

She was making the tea. 'The papers keep on saying this horrible war is nearly over, Jimmy' she said over her shoulder, 'so, please God, you'll never get caught up in it again.'

O'Neill remembered the time they met in the hospital in Portsmouth. Norma had made a similar wish then and he finished up at the invasions of Sicily and Normandy. Maybe she's got it right this time. He fervently hoped so anyway. Somehow, he felt totally drained. He wanted no more of this war.

For the next three months O'Neill felt that maybe Norma's prayers on his behalf were bearing fruit. When he returned to Portsmouth barracks after visiting Hoskins, it was a pleasant surprise to discover that he wasn't assigned to any department for duty. His not to reason why, he decided, so he discreetly kept his head down and lived in happy luxury in the Petty Officers' Mess. The war was, apparently, going well without him and air raids no longer disturbed the peace of the Portsmouth nights.

The Drafting Office seemed to have forgotten that Petty Officer Jimmy O'Neill was still a serving member of His Majesty's Royal Navy. He drew his pay and his rum and his duty-free cigarettes and spent his days in the Mess reading the papers and drinking satisfying pints of beer. At night he went dancing at the South Parade Pier. He had money in the bank and he lived life as a gentleman should.

Unfortunately, the call eventually came for him to report to the Drafting Office. Next day, to his horror and surprise, he was kitted out like a soldier in khaki battledress jacket and trousers and heavy studded boots. He was issued with a standard Colt 45 revolver and told that now he was the Supply Petty Officer in charge of the stores in Naval Party 120. The party, comprising 9 officers, 80 ratings and 20 marines was under the command of Captain Strong RN. They were to prepare to enter Europe attached to a regiment of the Polish army, their objective to take and hold the submarine base in Oderhaven, Germany.

'Capture the submarine base in Oderhaven? They must be fucking joking,' O'Neill gasped to his new opposite number, Petty Officer Writer Mark Roberts. They were two of a group of 40, each laden with 30 pounds of equipment, gasping their way on a ten-mile route march designed to get them physically fit for the combat duties which lay ahead. 'Naval Party 120 couldn't fight its way out of a fucking wet paper bag.'

For the next four months, they were shunted in ships and lorries from Dover to Antwerp to Borg Leopold and back to Brussels. They were loaded like surplus baggage on to American Dakotas and finally dumped in Oldenburg airport. In all that time, the weary khaki-clad sailors of Naval Party 120 had never heard a shot fired in anger. They began to wonder why they'd bothered to come. Then suddenly the good times were over.

I don't believe this is happening to me, O'Neill thought miserably. The full weight of Petty Officer Writer Mark Roberts's body, lying on top of him, held him firmly wedged in the narrow ditch into which they had thrown themselves.

Minutes before, they were relaxing peacefully in the back of a truck loaded with boxes and bales of naval stores and clothing. Theirs was one of a convoy of twenty trucks carrying Naval Party 120 and their equipment along the coast road leading to the German submarine base at Oderhaven. About ten miles ahead they occasionally heard the distant din of battle when forward units of the Polish Army engaged the retreating German forces.

On the afternoon of May 6, 1945, Roberts was giving O'Neill a lecture on the basics of high finance. Roberts had been an Assistant Manager in Barclay's Bank before he was conscripted. Though the pater could have wangled him a commission, he had elected to serve on the lower deck. He wanted to be a stoker but higher powers decided that with his experience he would serve the cause of freedom better as a Writer looking after the pay and secretarial affairs of the navy.

'Tobacco is the new currency of Europe, dear boy,' he emphasised to O'Neill, 'with the humble bar of chocolate playing a minor role. So he who controls the supply of tobacco also controls the major supply of finance,' He looked meaningfully into O'Neill's face. 'I do hope, dear boy, that when you indented for our supplies back in dear old England you had the good sense to ensure that we are carrying an adequate supply of.. er.. finance.'

O'Neill smiled enigmatically, his eyes closed. He was remembering a story Chief Mullins told him. As an innocent Leading Supply Assistant in charge of a cruiser's Slop Room on the Far Eastern Station, they had docked in Shanghai.

'Would you believe it,' the Chief asked him, 'every fucking raincoat I had in that store was size 3 or 4 and everybody knows that a Chinaman is only size 0.' The Chief had shaken his head at his own stupidity in not carrying out a comprehensive research study of the potential Chinese market in raincoats. The lesson had not been lost on O'Neill. Naval Party 120 was carrying three times the amount of tobacco they would normally carry.

Mark Robert's finance lecture was suddenly interrupted by the throbbing whine of a diving Messerschmitt. The noise was earsplitting and Roberts and O'Neill and their driver had barely time to scramble into the wet ditch before the plane swept back for a second attacking run over the convoy of lorries.

O'Neill cringed even tighter within himself when the whistle and whine of ricocheting shells and bullets splattered on the concrete roadway. Then, as suddenly as the attack began, it was over. Blissful quiet once again enveloped the flat German countryside. The lone Messerschmitt, its fuel nearly exhausted, headed back to base.

Two of the convoy's trucks were burning fiercely. Four bodies lay slumped in pools of blood on the road.

When O'Neill clawed his way out of the ditch, he knuckled dirty water and mud out of his eyes. Mark Roberts removed his spectacles and carefully cleaned them with a handkerchief. He was looking pointedly at O'Neill's battledress trousers.

'James, dear boy,' he asked, his voice concerned, 'did you piss yourself or what?' O'Neill looked down at his mud-stained battledress.

'I'm fucked if I know,' he said, sighing, 'and at this stage I'm fucked if I care either.'

He looked up and down the road. Mud-covered figures were hauling themselves out of the flooded ditches. He unstrapped the webbing belt and the holster and flung them in disgust into the back of the lorry. Then he scrubbed inadequately at his battledress with a handful of grass. 'What worries me is how the hell a man of my experience could allow himself to get into this mess in the first place.'

He strapped on the revolver again. The dead were hurriedly buried and the convoy trundled forward. Dawn would see them at the gates of Oderhaven. Their moment of truth was at hand and they weren't looking forward to it. But that evening fate intervened with the announcement that the war in Europe was over. Germany had surrendered unconditionally. Oderhaven was taken without a shot being fired.

At 1700 hours on the afternoon of May 7th, Naval Party 120 occupied the submarine base, a group of three four-storey buildings in the dockyard. The Germans had been given one hour to pack what they could carry before being marched off to a prisoner-of-war camp hastily set up on the outskirts of the town. Though Oderhaven itself was devastated by years of RAF and American attacks, not one bomb had hit the barracks.

At 1800 hours an enterprising marine on the prowl discovered that the basement of Block Three was packed with crates of liquor. By 19.00 hours before Captain Strong found out what was happening and ordered an armed guard to be placed on the cellar, most of the members of Naval Party 120 had lost interest in the war.

O'Neill and Roberts managed to get three cases of Dutch gin to their cabins and were happily flaked out on comfortable beds for the first time in five months. Thank you, Norma pet, O'Neill thought happily, you got it right at last. I'll be home before you know it. I'll write you a long letter tonight. He took a gurgling swig at the gin bottle and rolled it round his mouth. For your next trick, Jimmy boy, he thought, keep your fucking head down and don't let anybody get you involved in the shagging war with Japan.

Chapter Fourteen

Germany

General Montgomery decreed that members of the Allied Forces were forbidden to fraternise in any way with the German people.

'That bloody man should have been a monk,' O'Neill remarked irreverently to Roberts. 'You know something? It's four and a half months since I even spoke to a woman, never mind getting my hands on one. And that was back somewhere in Belgium.' They were returning to the submarine barracks, now renamed Royal Nelson barracks, after an evening spent drinking warm beer in the newly-opened Sergeants' Club - one of the few bars in Oderhaven not destroyed by Allied bombs. It was well past the curfew hour and the streets were deserted.

'I know, dear boy, I know,' said Roberts sadly, 'I was with you, remember? She offered us a quick job each for one miserable bloody bar of chocolate and we didn't have one. And she was absolutely gorgeous as I recall.' He shook his head in disgust and fingered the bar of chocolate in his pocket. He would never be caught out like that again.

There were no streetlights and even though a bright moon picked out the gaunt skeletons of the bombed buildings all around them, they still had to pick their way carefully along the rubble-strewn pavements. O'Neill stopped abruptly and grasped Roberts by the arm.

'Do you hear music?' he whispered. Roberts cocked his head to one side and listened. Then faintly through the darkness they heard the tinny sound of a gramophone playing.

'It's coming from down there,' Roberts said at last, pointing at a dimly lit window on the ground floor of a three-storey building beside the railway station. Most of the windows were boarded up. They groped their way across the street and down the alleyway and stood listening outside the window. They could hear the sound of laughter and there was some clapping when the music stopped.

'There's a party going on in there,' whispered O'Neill, 'and by the sound of things they're dancing and if they're dancing there must be women.' He looked at Roberts. 'What d'you reckon? Will we join the party? I say fuck Montgomery and his stupid non-frat policy. We're not in his shagging army, anyhow, so who the hell is he to tell us what to do?'

Roberts thought about it briefly and then nodded in agreement. The music started again. 'Point taken, old man,' he said. He belched warm beer. 'Anyway, it's up to m'Lords at the Admiralty to instruct us naval bods on our copulation choices.' He knocked loudly on the window pane. 'If we want a bit of frat then we're entitled to it. Who knows? These German chappies might even have something half decent to drink.'

The music stopped abruptly and the light in the room was switched off. Roberts looked at O'Neill and shook his head. Suddenly, everything had gone quiet. O'Neill knocked on the window again. Then he saw the curtains parting slightly and the dim outline of a woman's head peeped out at them. He smiled at her.

'May we join the party?' he called. 'May we come in, there's just the two of us...'

The curtains closed and they could hear the agitated voice of the woman speaking to the others in the room. Then the light was switched on again. A minute or so later they heard a door opening just a few yards farther up the street.

'If you wish, you may come in, please,' a woman's voice invited.

O'Neill's heart did a little jump when he saw her in the light of the hallway. She was tall, blonde and bronzed from the sun and she went in and out in all the right places. He introduced himself and Mark Roberts. As she led them along the corridor he admired the way her bottom waggled from side to side under the tight floral frock.

Roberts made appealing signs to O'Neill. 'Please, Jimmy,' he whispered, 'leave this one to me,' This blonde beauty was going to be his territory. And fuck Montgomery.

She stopped at the door of the room, noticing for the first time that they were wearing revolvers. She pointed at them distastefully indicating that they should take them off and hang them on the hooks provided for coats in the hall.

The music started again. She opened the door and led them into the crowded room. There was a mixed group of about twenty men and women, some dancing some standing with glasses of wine in their hands. All eyes turned and stared curiously at them. O'Neill felt his face going red. Roberts shuffled uncomfortably. After being at war with them for five years, he thought, this is the first time I've come face to face with the German enemy. The blonde's eyes held his and he saw that they were a delightful shade of brown. She took their arms and led them to a table holding bottles of wine.

'I'm Renata,' she smiled, 'and these are my family and some friends. We are having a welcome home party for my brother-in-law.' She poured out two glasses of red wine for them. 'This was the best hotel in Oderhaven before the war. My father owns it, and his father before him laid down an excellent cellar many years ago. He is now long dead but if you appreciate good wine, you will love this.'

Roberts swirled the wine gently in the glass, sniffing the fruity bouquet before sipping slowly. His face lit up in delight as he allowed the wine to roll around in his mouth savouring the flavour appreciatively.

'Dear lady,' he said at last, bowing to Renata and tapping his glass to hers in a toast. 'This is truly an excellent vintage. I drink to your dear departed grandad. May he be granted eternal peace in that great wine cellar in the sky.' Renata looked at him, slightly bemused.

O'Neill squeezed her arm. 'Don't mind him. All English public school boys talk like that At the back of it all he's harmless when you get to know him.'

The music stopped and O'Neill saw the piano in the corner of the room. He drained his glass and walked over to it. He hadn't played a piano since the night he had serenaded Norma briefly in the YMCA in Liverpool. Christ, he thought guiltily, I promised I'd write to her and I forgot again. I'll have to remember tomorrow...

He sat down and his fingers explored caressingly over the keys. At least it's in tune, he thought, I'd better give them something German. He closed his eyes and the haunting notes of Beethoven's Moonlight Sonata flowed out of him. The chatter in the room died to an appreciative silence.

When he finished there was loud applause and demands for an encore. Without thinking. O'Neill found himself playing Maria Elena. Norma's face haunted his mind, his heart full of his love. The dancing couples swayed all round him. O'Neill was in his element but he knew from years of bitter experience that if the pianist were mug enough he'd be left sitting at the instrument all night while the others enjoyed the party. That wasn't what he'd come here for. There were more calls for an encore.

'Later, 'O'Neill waved, standing up and bowing. 'I'll give you more later.'

There was a small silver tray holding six silver goblets on top of the piano. O'Neill picked up one of the goblets and examined it curiously. It was plain with no markings and it didn't seem to be antique. He felt eyes on him and looked up. Roberts was engaged in animated conversation with Renata, his hand holding hers, his eyes alight with an interest that O'Neill had never seen before. The man sitting at the table with them he guessed was the brother-in-law. He was watching O'Neill intently. O'Neill felt himself going scarlet. Does he think I'm going to pinch the bloody things, he thought, suddenly annoyed.

He replaced the goblet and went to the wine table to replenish his empty glass and then looked around the room to size up whatever female talent there might be on offer. Roberts and Renata got up to dance. O'Neill decided to join the brother-in-law at his table.

'Good evening,' he said, 'my name's O'Neill - Jimmy, for short.' He pointed back at the piano. 'And I wasn't aiming to steal the family silver. I was just admiring it.'

The man stood up and offered his hand. 'Good evening, *Mein Herr*,' he said, bowing politely, 'I'm Herman Beck, and I apologise if you thought that - that...' His voice trailed off when he saw the sudden puzzled look on O'Neill's face.

'Do I know you?' O'Neill asked, his brow furrowing. 'Have we met before?'

The man sat down, his face suddenly concerned. He swallowed the remainder of his drink and then shook his head, smiling. 'It -it's not possible that we could have ever met,' he said. He topped up his glass and sipped at it. 'I've never been to England. We couldn't have met...'

As if a light had switched on inside his head, O'Neill saw the picture suddenly clearing in his mind - the choppy waters of the Mediterranean, the cold dawn sky, the submarine towering over the carley float, the barrel of the machine gun menacing down on Hoskins and himself. His mouth went dry.

'Jesus, I don't believe this,' he said. He gulped the wine. 'No, it wasn't in England.' His voice had dropped to a whisper. 'It was in the Med in August '42, the convoy to Malta, remember? You were the captain of the sub that sunk the Pinewell. You surfaced beside a carley float the morning after. Me and my mate were on it.'

Beck's face turned grey. He took a handkerchief from his pocket and blew his nose. At last he looked up again, his blue eyes meeting O'Neill's.

'When you were examining the goblets I thought your face was vaguely familiar. That's why I was staring.' He looked around the room and then back to O'Neill. He sighed deeply. 'What - what do you propose to do about me?'

O'Neill drained his glass again. 'What do I propose to do about you?' he asked. 'I'll tell you what I propose to do about you.' He held out his hand. 'I propose to shake your hand and thank you now that I've been given the opportunity. From stories I've heard, there were plenty of U-boat captains out there who blasted survivors boats out of the water and they would gladly have done that to Hoskie and me if they had the chance.' He grinned. 'Don't you remember? I thought that's what you were going to do that morning...'

Beck's face broke into a relieved smile. 'Then - then you don't intend to report me to the authorities? Needless to say, I don't go around telling everybody I sank a British aircraft carrier...' He wiped his lips with the handkerchief and looked to where Roberts and Renata were dancing. 'There - there are so many rumours of trials for so called atrocities... war crimes, they call them.... to be held at Nuremberg. I was afraid.... it is hard for people like me to understand what might now be called a war crime...' He sighed and pointed with his glass at the tray and goblets on the piano. 'Did you know that U-boat captains were awarded a silver goblet for each successful mission up to six and then if they managed to survive a seventh mission they got the silver tray to complete the set?' His eyes held O'Neill's in a steady stare. 'That tray was awarded to me when I returned here to Oderhaven after sinking the Pinewell.' He shrugged and topped up their two glasses from the wine bottle.

O'Neill touched his to Beck's in a toast. 'Your good health,' he said. 'We both had jobs to do, and we did them as best we could. We can't be blamed for that now.' He was thinking of the Messerschmitt he had shot down over the

Bristol Channel. 'As far as I'm concerned, the bloody war is over and the fact that you and I met before - well, that's between you and me. I won't mention it again - not even to Roberts or Renata if that's the way you want it.'

Roberts and Renata were dancing a slow foxtrot, her arms about his neck, his cheek touching hers, his eyes gazing soulfully into heaven.

O'Neill shook his head in mock despair. 'You know something, Herman,' he said, 'I do believe poor old Mark Roberts has been trapped by the first German fraulein he's ever met.'

Herman Beck smiled and nodded. 'My sister-in-law is a very attractive lady,' he said, 'and also a very determined woman when she knows what she wants,' He stood up. 'Come and meet my wife, Irma. She's with her father in the kitchen, preparing some food for the guests - not that there is very much available, I'm afraid...'

O'Neill felt embarrassed. 'Nothing for Mark and me, thank you. Herman,' he said. 'We're enjoying the party but we don't need food. In fact, if I'd known we were coming I could have brought some along.'

Herman touched the 'S' in the gold star on O'Neill's sleeve. 'What does this mean?' he asked, 'we don't have such a marking in the Kreigmarine.'

'Supply branch,' O'Neill told him. 'We are responsible for all supplies, food, rum, clothing, tobacco...'

The German was obviously very interested. 'Tobacco? You are responsible for stores of tobacco?' He touched his hand to his mouth. 'Now that is interesting...'

Over the following months Renata and Roberts fell deeply in love. The friendship between O'Neill and Herman Beck blossomed into a thriving business partnership. Beck, through a wide circle of ex-German officer colleagues, had a contact network that reached right through the British and American Zones. O'Neill, with a ready supply of tobacco available to him, provided the hard currency.

On the political front too there were many changes. The war against Japan finished in August and the buzz on the impatient lower deck was that demobilisation for all hostilities-only personnel was imminent. To hasten the process, Montgomery's non-fraternisation decree was lifted and it was now official policy to employ Germans in non-key positions in the barracks whenever possible. The able-seaman detailed to help O'Neill in the Clothing Store had already been demobbed. A German army ex-corporal, Franz Greer, was employed to replace him. In addition to his store duties, Franz also became O'Neill's personal valet.

After a whirlwind courtship Roberts and Renata officially announced their engagement at a family party in the newly opened refurbished Hotel Kaiser. Next morning, Franz stood to attention beside O'Neill's bed and coughed discreetly. O'Neill stirred and grunted but didn't wake. Franz placed the tray holding O'Neill's breakfast of bacon, eggs, sausages and toast on the locker beside the bed and coughed more loudly. O'Neill's eyes opened blearily and he looked up at Franz. He rubbed his hand across his throbbing forehead and wrinkled his nose as the smell of the food wafted under his nostrils. Franz's heels clicked together.

'*Guten morgan, mein Chief,*' he said, 'it is 8 o'clock. I have brought your breakfast from the mess.'

O'Neill lifted his head and looked at the plate. Then he turned his face to the wall. 'For God's sakes, Franz,' he groaned in misery, 'you know I don't want that shite - you eat it.' O'Neill went back to sleep.

When Franz finished eating, he laid out freshly laundered underwear, socks and a white shirt on the end of the bed. O'Neill's uniform, which he had dropped on the floor the night before, had already been brushed and pressed and placed on a hanger. Franz checked through the bundle of notes he found in O'Neill's pocket and separated the sterling and dollar notes from the marks and placed them in three piles on the dressing-table. Then he glanced at his watch and waited. At 08.45, he coughed loudly again and when he got no response he shook O'Neill gently by the shoulder.

'Sorry, Chief,' he said when O'Neill's eyes flickered open, 'but it is time for you to get up now. The fraulein who is to start working with you today will be arriving at the store in a few minutes.'

O'Neill stared at him uncomprehendingly and then sighed and stretched himself. 'My God, I'd forgotten all about her,' he said miserably. He heaved himself out of the bed and sat naked on the edge of it, his head in his hands. It had been one helluva party. Franz helped him into a black silk dressing-gown and then knelt down and eased his feet into a pair of velvet slippers.

O'Neill sighed again. 'Like a good man, Franz,' he said, 'take the keys of the store and go down and open up. Tell her to wait in the office till I get there. Okay?' He looked at his watch. 'Give her a cup of tea or something. I'll be along in a half an hour or so.' Then he headed for the bathroom to shave and shower.

When the war finished, Fraulein Lorelie Brunner was 18 years old and still attending school. Because she could speak fluent English the burgomeister's office had instructed her to report for duty at the Clothing Store in the Royal Nelson barracks. She had no idea what the work entailed. She kept pulling her skirt nervously over her knees as she sat waiting in the office. Her mother had warned her bluntly that she should keep her legs crossed at all times when dealing with the Englanders.

'We may have lost the war, *liebchen*,' she warned her only daughter, 'but we don't have to lose our pride as well so never open your legs to the Englanders. That's what they'll want from our German women. They always did and they always will - the Russians, the French, the English, they're all the same. And our dear Fuehrer would have expected more of us.'

Lorelei stood up and lifted her skirt high to her thighs to readjust and tighten her suspenders. She ran her hand down along the backs of her legs, straightening the seams of her stockings. She sat down quickly and crossed her legs when she heard footsteps approaching the office door. Her heart gave a nervous lurch when O'Neill appeared. She stood up, acutely aware that his eyes were sweeping appreciatively over her body. She drew herself to her full 5 feet 4 inches and forced her lips into a smile.

'I am Lorelei Brunner,' she told him, 'and I was told to report to Petty Officer O'Neill in the Clothing Store.' She handed him the card given to her at the burgomeister's office. O'Neill glanced at it and nodded. Lorelei's smart linen suit hugged her slight slim figure. Long auburn hair curled around a pretty face, and the wide mouth with its voluptuous lips was, O'Neill decided, full of wonderful promise. If he'd been allowed to choose a secretary for himself, he thought happily, he couldn't have done better.

'Well, I'm O'Neill and this is the Clothing Store so you're in the right place, Lorelei,' he said. He repeated her name. 'Lorelei. That's a lovely name.' Lorelei blushed and he grinned. 'So if you're finished your tea we might as well start with a conducted tour of the stores.'

Every fortnight, the personnel of Royal Nelson were paid in German marks. Each man was entitled to buy one pound of duty-free tobacco on the first day of the month. One day's pay bought the tobacco which could then be sold on the black market for the equivalent of a year's pay. So everybody in Royal Nelson was extremely rich by ordinary naval standards. The snag of course, was that, apart from the canteen and the clothing store, there was no place to spend the money and it couldn't be brought back to England.

Expensive champagne dinners could be bought in the canteen. On the three days each week when the clothing store opened for business, long queues formed and everybody bought everything and anything that was in stock. Whether the items fitted or not didn't seem to matter.

'Keeping the office accounts and the books up to date will be your job,' O'Neill told Lorelie. 'Nowadays, this store is so busy all the time I just can't keep up with it.'

He opened the door of the clothing store and switched on the lights. Lorelei's eyes widened. Shelf after shelf of shirts, underwear, socks, shoes, handkerchiefs, pyjamas, towels, all those wonderful things that she had never seen in the shops of wartime Germany were stacked high from floor to ceiling.

In the bedding store she surreptitiously fingered the quality of the pure white wool blankets, the linen sheets and the pillowcases. But it was the tobacco store that absolutely took her breath away.

'Is - is all this tabac - tobacco?' she asked in disbelief pointing at the cardboard cartons stacked to the ceiling. O'Neill nodded. When Naval Party 120 was formed he had created an extra mess in the books in which he had victualled thirty phantom seamen thus ensuring that he himself would always have a plentiful supply of tobacco for his own use. He allowed Corporal Duffy, the marine in charge of the Motor Pool, an extra pound of tobacco per month in return for a guarantee that O'Neill would have a car and driver at his disposal at all times. Petty Officer Writer Mark Roberts was allowed an extra three pounds of tobacco a month. In return, he arranged for all of O'Neill's pay to be allotted to a deposit account in a bank in Portsmouth. Neither of them had drawn any pay since they arrived in Germany. It had all been banked in England. Franz was paid one tin per month for his valeting duties.

Herman Beck had established contact with a dealer in the American Zone. Beck bought up such black market items as cameras, fur coats and jewellery for tobacco supplied by O'Neill and passed them on to his contact who disposed of them to American servicemen for dollars. After deducting his commission Beck, paid off O'Neill in dollars.

Lorelei picked up one of the sealed tins of cigarette tobacco and examined it curiously. She was standing quite close to O'Neill. Despite the overpowering aroma of tobacco that pervaded the storeroom he could smell the warm perfume of her body. Their hands touched when she handed back the tin.

'Over here is where we keep the pipe tobacco,' O'Neill told her. He tried to squeeze past her in the narrow passageway between the stacked cartons of tobacco. She was facing him. O'Neill hesitated when his body touched against her feeling the full length of her from the firm thighs to the roundness of her belly and breasts. Lorelei smiled. He put his hands on her shoulders. She lifted her head and looked up at him, her moist lips parted, her breathing quickening. He pulled her close, his hands dropping down to the firm cheeks of her bottom straining under the tight skirt. Her small breasts jutted against him.

'You - you don't have to do anything like this,' O'Neill whispered. 'All you have to do is keep the books.'

Lorelei pressed against him. She could feel his hard erection between them.

'Chief!' It was Franz calling urgently from the office. 'Are you down the store, Chief? There's a telephone call from the Paymaster Lieutenant...'

O'Neill's mouth tightened and he sighed. Lorelei pulled back. O'Neill's hands tightened on her bottom and patted it gently. He dropped a quick kiss on the tip of her nose and then hurried up the corridor to the office.

Lorelei waited to compose herself. She picked up the tin of tobacco and weighed it speculatively in her hand. Mein Gott, she thought, for a moment or two there I quite forgot to keep my legs crossed and I've only been five minutes with the Englander. I must be more careful. She sighed and smiled. Whatever would *mutti* think of me? Or the Fuehrer!

Frau Brunner was torn with anxiety. It was half past seven in the evening and Lorelei still wasn't home after her first day's work with the Englanders. It was three kilometres walk from the Royal Nelson barracks to the block of flats where they lived and Lorelei should have been home by 6 o'clock at the latest.

The flat, comprising a small kitchen, an adjoining room with two beds and a tiny bathroom, was on the third floor. Her husband, a sergeant in the Wehrmacht had been killed on the Russian front.

Frau Brunner sat at the bedroom window, a coat around her shoulders to keep out the cold, and looked out at the heavy rain splattering on the dark roadway.

At eight o'clock a black Mercedes stopped outside the block of flats. *Frau* Brunner's heart thudded anxiously. SS officers used such cars in the old days. She held the curtains apart and peered anxiously into the dark. A man in a peaked cap got out of the Mercedes and walked around to the passenger door. He opened a large black umbrella to shield his passenger from the rain. *Frau* Brunner sighed in relief when she saw Lorelei getting out of the car. The driver handed Lorelei the umbrella and she made a dash to the door of the flats. He lifted out a large suitcase from the boot of the car and followed her.

The lift hadn't worked for months and *Frau* Brunner stood anxiously waiting for Lorelei at the open door of the flat. After a few minutes she arrived, the man in the peaked cap following behind her, the suitcase in his hand.

'Oh, Lorelei, *liebchen*, I was so worried..'

Lorelei dropped a reassuring kiss on her mother's cheek. The man put down the case. Lorelei smiled gratefully at him. '*Danke*, Hans,' she said, 'you are very kind.'

He bowed and touched his hand to his cap in salute. 'I do what the Chief tells me, *fraulein*,' he said. He bowed to *Frau* Brunner and went back down the stairs.

Frau Brunner's eyebrows lifted in question. 'Who is this Hans person?' she asked, suspicion tinging her voice, 'and who owns the car that brought you home?'

Lorelei's eyes were shining. She lifted the heavy suitcase onto the bed. *Frau* Brunner's breath gasped in her throat. Like a magician taking goodies from a magic hat, Lorelei lifted out a white wool blanket, a tin of tobacco, three large tins of corned beef, a paper bag full of tea, another full of sugar, six tins of condensed milk and a packet of Senior Service cigarettes.

Her mother drew back from her in horror. 'Lorelei,' she whispered, tears threatening in her voice, 'what have you done? Where did you get this? Who - who gave you all this stuff? You didn't.. you didn't...?'

Lorelei's hard gaze met hers. The smile was gone. 'I didn't what, *mutti?*' she asked. She unfolded the blanket and swung it around her shoulders, draping it like a long cape. 'This is a pure wool blanket, *mutti*,' she whispered defiantly, her voice hardening. 'It can be dyed - I'd suggest a light pastel blue - and there's enough material in it to make us two warm coats for the Winter.' She indicated the tin of tobacco and the tins of food. 'Why should we have to be always hungry, always wondering where the next meal will come from?' *Frau*

Brunner had slumped down on the bed, tears filling her eyes. Her worst suspicions were being confirmed. 'Oh, Lorelei, Lorelei, *liebchen*,' she sobbed, 'after all I told you, after all my warnings to you, surely you didn't...' She looked up pleadingly. 'Tell me, *liebchen*, you didn't - you didn't open your legs to an Englander, did you? Not on your first day working for them?'

Lorelei sighed and sat beside her mother on the bed, her arms hugging around her comfortingly. 'No, no *mutti*,' she whispered, trying desperately to reassure her, 'I didn't open my legs to an Englander.' She sighed and dabbed at her mother's eyes with a handkerchief. 'But I did open my legs to an Irelander, and *mutti*, it wasn't like you said it would be, ugly and horrible and degrading. It wasn't like that at all.' She hugged her mother tightly. 'He was gentle and kind and it was all so lovely and wonderful and beautiful.' She sighed, a matter-of-fact hardness creeping into her voice. 'Unfortunately, he got word this morning that he'll be returning to England in a few weeks time. That's why I couldn't afford to wait.'

Herman Beck was shocked when O'Neill told him that he'd shortly be leaving Germany to be demobbed from the navy.

'*Gott in Himmel*, Jimmy!' he grumbled, opening a bottle of wine. 'Just when we were getting our operation on a firm business-like footing.'

O'Neill, Roberts and Beck were sitting in the hotel lounge. Beck filled the three crystal glasses. 'Only today my man in Bonn was telling me that he now has contacts through Switzerland and any amount of cash in any currency can be paid through a Swiss bank to banks in England. Think of the potential such an arrangement could open up for you. And now they're pulling you out. Could you not sign on as a regular and volunteer to stay here?' He appealed to Roberts. 'Talk him into staying, Mark.'

O'Neill wasn't sure how he felt about being demobbed. All he knew was that after five years of war, most of it at sea, he'd had enough. No way would he ever consider signing on the regular navy. The petty discipline which controlled sailors' lives, he found irritating and ridiculous. Ever since New York when he had stumbled briefly into the high life of the financially independent, he had known exactly what he wanted. He wanted enough money to be independent. That's what he had here in Germany. But to return to England and be equally independent in a mixed-up post-war society was the immediate problem. He thought of Norma Perkins and their child in Liverpool and he sighed into the wine. More then anything else, he wanted to marry Norma and be a father to his child.

Mark Roberts lit a cigar, his brow furrowed. He knew from letters he'd seen passing across the Paymaster's desk that a new type currency was soon to be introduced to pay the Occupation Forces. That would put an end to the lucrative deals being made on the black market using German marks. It even meant that he and O'Neill would be forced to draw their pay!

'What you need now, Jimmy dear boy,' he said at last, 'is one really big deal that will pay off enough sterling or dollars to set you up comfortably in your own business when you get back to Blighty.' He blew a perfect smoke ring and stuck his finger into it till it floated away.

O'Neill nodded and sighed. Easier said than done, he thought. He still had that thousand pounds in the bank in Portsmouth, plus what he had added to it since he came to Germany. But if only he could get his hands on a decent amount of capital he and Hoskins, in partnership, could do wonders with the shop after he was demobbed.

Roberts sipped at his glass. 'You know that little scam you have going with a phantom mess and 30 phantom sailors?'

O'Neill shook his head. 'That stuff is small change, Mark,' he said. 'You can see what we make out of it every month. It's okay but - well, we've drained it dry...'

'Hear me out, dear boy,' Roberts interrupted. 'What I was about to suggest was not an extension of the phantom mess, no.' He sipped thoughtfully at his wine. Beck was watching him impatiently. 'What I had in mind was...' He paused for effect and looked cautiously around the empty lounge, his voice dropping to a whisper. 'What I had in mind was, in fact, a phantom naval party of one hundred and twenty or so officers and men.'

O'Neill and Beck stiffened in their chairs. 'Jesus,' said O'Neill.

'*Gott in Himmel*!' said Herman Beck. He topped up the glasses and lit a cigarette. 'Go on, Mark.'

'You create this phantom party,' Roberts said slowly, working out the details in his head as he went along, 'and you base it in a phantom seaport and you go down to Antwerp with a real lorry and you draw a full supply of real bedding, clothing and tobacco, cutlery and so on to cover the needs of these 120 officers and men. You hand it all over to Herman here for disposal and -' He paused, his long experience in the world of banking making him suddenly cautious. He turned to his future brother-in-law.

'Dear boy, with all due respects to our future relationship after Renata and I are allowed to get married, I must insist on Jimmy's behalf that a proper contract be drawn up. You'll have to agree a fair market price and this chappie of yours in Bonn will have to deposit the money in advance in the pater's bank in London. Otherwise there will be no deal.' He patted O'Neill's knee. 'Now there would be a killing worthy of your devious talents, Jimmy, dear boy. And it would set you up for life..'

Over the next weeks Beck and O'Neill planned Operation Final Fling with military precision. The phantom Naval Party was based in a phantom barracks, HMS Royal Pinewell.

'As we were both so deeply involved with Pinewell earlier in our careers,' Beck remarked drily, 'it would seem to be an appropriate title. And we'll base it at...' He thought for a few moments. 'How about Freirsburghaven? There's no such place but...'

The list of stores was drawn up and a price agreed at £10,000 sterling. Beck took charge of planning and organisation. Within a week one of his many underground contacts had provided him with a rubber date stamp bearing the legend 'HMS Royal Pinewell, Freirsburghaven' and two forged Pay Books, one for a Supply Petty Officer John Smith and the other for a Royal Marine, Tom Taylor. Herman had insisted that he should come along as driver, so he became a Royal Marine.

Four tins of tobacco for Corporal Duffy expedited the quick transfer of one 3-ton truck to HMS Royal Pinewell based in Freirsburghaven.

'Where's this Freirsburghaven place?' Duffy asked, making out and signing the necessary transfer forms.

'Fifty miles or so up the coast,' O'Neill answered vaguely. 'They've no Supply staff so I got landed with the job. Just my bloody luck. As if I hadn't enough to do down here. I've got one of their Jerry drivers with me, so if you just make sure her tank is full we'll be on our way. Okay?'

When word came though from Mark's father that a lodgment of £10,000 had been transferred from a Swiss bank into a new account opened in the name of one Mr. James O'Neill, O'Neill smiled his relief. Things were taking shape at last.

'I must say, dear boy, that those horn-rimmed spectacles make quite a fetching disguise,' Roberts told O'Neill, 'but I do think Herman's Royal Marine moustache is a little over the top.'

It was 0600 hours and Beck and O'Neill were in the truck outside the Hotel Kaiser. It was still dark when they set off on the long road to Antwerp, 150 miles away. Operation Final Fling was on.

They arrived at the naval stores in Antwerp at 16.00 hours and O'Neill handed in the signed and stamped Demand Notes for the supplies to HMS Royal Pinewell. His heart was thumping in case somebody recognised him but after a cursory check of his documentation he was told to report back at 10.00 hours next morning.

'We've got to make sure that we keep out of the way of the Military Police,' O'Neill whispered to Beck as they drank a glass of beer in a back-street cafe. 'We don't want anybody asking us stupid questions so we'll just have one or two more and then we'll kip down for the night in the back of the truck.'

Next morning at 10.00 hours O'Neill once again presented himself at the Stores. Within an hour the truck was loaded and they were on their way out of Antwerp by midday.

When they were twenty kilometres from the German border Beck turned to O'Neill, a happy smile on his face. 'I wish the other operation you and I were involved in together down in the Med had gone as smoothly as this one. It was, as the Englanders say, a piece of cake.' He laughed and was about to peel the false moustache from his lip when two heavy motor-bikes pulled out of a lay-by and chased after them, sirens screaming.

O'Neill's heart stopped. Beck looked in his mirror. 'Military Police,' he groaned. He looked at O'Neill. 'It's only twenty kilometres to the German border. Will we make a run for it?'

O'Neill shook his head, trying to think. Just when everything was going his way - the fucking war over, money in the bank, his future with Norma and the kids assured, and now it could all blow up in his face... 'No, Herman,' he said, his voice a whisper. The motor-bikes were coming abreast of them. 'I'll bluff it out, and for Christ sake, you keep your fucking German mouth shut.'

The Military Police sergeant waved them down. Beck brought the truck to a halt. O'Neill leaned out the window, his face in a broad smile. 'What can I do for you, sergeant?'

The sergeant ignored him and went to the back of the truck and looked in. Then he came back to O'Neill. 'Let's see the documentation to cover this lot,' he demanded.

O'Neill handed over the Supply Notes. 'You'll find them all in order, sergeant,' he said. 'We drew this lot this morning at the Naval Stores in Antwerp.'

The sergeant read down the list and seemed satisfied. 'You know you're supposed to have an armed escort with you, Jack, or do you?' he asked. 'This area is noted for highway robberies. There are gangs of fucking refugees of all nationalities around here and they'd steal anything that isn't tied down.' He gestured to his colleague sitting on the other bike. 'Right Jonnie, we'll escort the Royal Navy to the German border. It'll fill in the afternoon for us.' He turned to O'Neill. 'Once into Germany, you're on your own, sailor. But make sure you bring an escort if you're coming this way again. You can't trust anybody any more now that the bloody war is over.'

Beck started up the truck. 'I'll remember that, sergeant,' O'Neill said gratefully, 'if I'm ever coming this way again. And thanks for the escort. It's much appreciated.' The sergeant rode in front and his colleague covered their rear. Beck was watching him in the driving mirror.

'Mein Gott, Jimmy, how could the Germans lose the war? Here we are - we steal thousands of pounds worth of British stores and they provide us with an armed escort to make sure we get away.' He shook his head. 'The English are so stupid. How did they ever win the war?'

O'Neill smiled, remembering the day the Gunner's Mate shot the seagull over the Solent. 'They've been at it a long time, Herman,' he said, 'and there's fuck-all to it when you knows what you're at.'

At 19.00 hours Beck parked the truck outside a warehouse on the outskirts of Oldenburgh. He heaved a tired but happy sigh. 'Like I was saying when the Military Police interrupted me,' he said, 'that was a piece of cake.'

O'Neill nodded happily. 'Right, Herman, let's get this lot unloaded and get ourselves back to Oderhaven,' He looked around. 'You've arranged for your people to meet us here...?

Beck took an envelope from his pocket. 'Have you forgotten that this truck was transferred to HMS Royal Pinewell?' he asked, 'As you are now the sole survivor of that unfortunate party I am making you an offer to buy the truck.' He handed the envelope to O'Neill. 'There's one hundred American dollars in there, Jimmy, and that's as good a price as you'll get for a clapped out old wagon like this.' He pointed at a black Mercedes parked discreetly on the other side of the road. 'Mark arranged for Hans to meet you here.'

They got out of the truck. Herman took O'Neill's hand and shook it warmly. 'I'm going on to Frankfurt with this lot and I'll be there for a couple of weeks.'

O'Neill's eyes widened. 'Two weeks? But - but that means we won't meet again,' he protested. 'You know I'm leaving Germany next week. You can't just walk away like this.'

Beck's arms closed around him in an affectionate bear hug. 'We were but ships that passed in the night, Jimmy,' he said. 'We both survived and now goodbye, Supply Petty Officer O'Neill. It was good knowing you.'

O'Neill felt a lump in his throat. He swallowed and then came to attention and saluted. 'Goodbye then Kapitanleutnant Beck,' he said. 'And thank you for everything. It was good knowing you too.'

Hans opened the Mercedes door for O'Neill. They sat and watched the lights of the truck move into the darkness. O'Neill sighed.

Hans handed him a silver hip flask. 'Chief Roberts told me to give you this,' he said. 'It's your two days rum ration. He said you'd probably need it.' O'Neill opened the flask, drained it in two gulps and flopped back in the seat.

'A good trip, Mein Herr?' Hans revved up the Mercedes. O'Neill looked at the money Herman Beck had given him for the truck.

'You could say that, Hans.' He put the hundred dollars in his pocket and closed his eyes wearily. Was this what life was really all about? 'You can take us home now, Hans' A picture of Norma Perkins with his children, little Tommy and baby Norma floated up in his mind. He sighed happily. I'm on my way at last, Norma darling, he thought. It took me a while but I'm coming home now to take care of you and the kids...

Chapter Fifteen

The End

The rain stopped before O'Neill reached the Green Man pub. Jesus, he thought, wouldn't you think they'd give us a raincoat with this lot? He still felt uncomfortable and conspicuous in the light grey suit, the spotted red tie and brown shoes issued to him when he was demobbed in Portsmouth. He changed the heavy suitcase from one hand to the other.

It was evening and he was surprised at how empty the bar was compared with the old days. He reached up to adjust his cap to its usual jaunty angle and realised that he wasn't wearing one. I'll never get used to this, he thought. Becoming a civvy overnight after seven years service in the navy wasn't easy. The lone barmaid eyed him, smiling. O'Neill ordered a glass of rum.

On the train journey from Portsmouth to Liverpool he'd gone over in his mind a dozen times how he'd propose to Norma, but he could still feel an unsure tingle in his stomach. How many times had he written? Twice! And he should have written to tell her he was coming. He should have written more often down the years – kept in touch with Hoskins. Anyway, he loved her. Christ, he'd been unfaithful to her so often, but she was the only one he ever really wanted. That he was sure of. And she loved him. They were meant for each other.

'Better make that a large one,' he said to the barmaid.

'Had a good war, sailor?' she asked him as she measured out the drink. He cocked his head to one side, surprised at the question. The barmaid laughed. 'I know you were a sailor, son,' she said, 'I'd recognise that navy demob outfit at fifty yards. Seen hundreds of 'em passing through here in the last few months.'

O'Neill had never thought of his war in terms of good or bad. Now he considered it, sipping slowly at the rum. Then he nodded. 'Yep, you could say I had a good war,' he told her. 'In fact, I'd say 'twas a very good war.' He drained the glass. And now things are going to get even better because I'm going to marry the only woman I ever loved.

'Could I leave the suitcase here for an hour or two?' he asked. 'I've got to meet a mate of mine I was in the navy with. We're going to set up a supermarket like I saw in America.' He handed in the case and she put it under the bar. 'And I'm going to get married! What d'ye think of that...?'

'Congratulations and I hope everything works out for you, son,' she smiled. 'It's not easy getting back to normal again. So much changed during the war...'

He swallowed another rum and left the pub. He felt much more confident now. The houses in Norma's street looked different with the streetlights on. He'd go straight to her place and call to Hoskie's shop later.

At first he thought there was nobody at home. He knocked again, louder. Then he heard the scramble of feet in the hall, the light was switched on and the door opened. The tense smile faded from O'Neill's face. A Royal Marine sergeant stood in the door. He was holding a struggling child by the hand and O'Neill smiled when he saw what seemed to be a small version of his own face staring up at him.

'What can I do for you, mate?' the sergeant asked impatiently, struggling to keep Tommy under control. 'This fella's a bit of a handful...'

'Yeah, I - I can see that,' O'Neill stuttered, searching for words.

The strained silence between them was shattered by the music of Maria Elena echoing loudly from the direction of the kitchen. The Sergeant's face went red. 'Jesus,' he said, 'her Granny'll kill her if she scratches that bloody record...' His voice rose to a shout. 'For God's sake, Norma, will you switch that gramophone off before you break it.' He turned to O'Neill, forcing a smile. 'Between herself and her mother they'd drive you mad playing that shagging record. It's getting to the state that I'll smash it meself one of these days.'

The music stopped and little Norma came running out. She looked up curiously at O'Neill. He smiled down at her.

'I - I was hoping to see -ah - Mrs. Perkins,' he said to the sergeant. 'She's - she's a friend - I used to be in digs here once. My pal Hoskie is married to her daughter Pearl....'

The sergeant's face broke into a smile. 'Ah, now I have you - you're O'Neill. Norma told me all about you and about the money that bought the shop...' He winked. 'Wish to Christ I knew a few canteen managers like George did.' O'Neill's hand was ruffling Tommy's hair. Jesus, he's a big lad for a two and a half year old ... 'And she told me about how you saved George's life down in the Med that time.'

'Ah, don't mind Mrs. Perkins,' O'Neill laughed. 'She exaggerates that thing a bit...'

'By the way,' the sergeant said, 'she's not Mrs. Perkins any more. We got married last month. She's Mrs. Jones now....'

Tommy had taken hold of O'Neill's hand. Little Norma was staring up at him with big blue eyes. O'Neill bent down to her trying to hide the shock on his face.

'Pearl's in hospital - she's just had another baby and George has gone to visit. That's why Norma isn't here just now. She's minding the shop. You could go down there. George should be home soon. They shut the shop at six....'

O'Neill gave Norma a kiss on the cheek and patted Tommy's head, keeping his face averted. He nodded. 'Yeah, that's what I'll do,' he said. 'That's what I'll do. I'll go down and say hello....' He waved, forcing a smile. 'Bye, Tommy. Bye Norma.' He held out his hand to the marine. 'Oh, and congratulations....'

Jesus, he thought, how could you do that, Norma? How could you marry that fucking leatherneck? Didn't you know we were meant for each other? Didn't you know I'd be back? Didn't I keep telling you? No, you didn't, you stupid bollix. It's your own fault. You never fucking wrote. You did fuck-all...

He stood in a doorway opposite the shop. He could see Norma behind the counter and his heart turned over. She was, if it were possible, more beautiful than ever. Tears were gathering in his eyes but he forced them back. Then he saw Hoskie limping down the street. He cowered back in the darkness of the doorway.

Hoskins went into the shop and Norma hugged her arms about him, their conversation animated. Hoskins looked at his watch and helped Norma into her coat. She came out and waited, standing under the street light. O'Neill hungered at the beauty of her, the slim figure, the hair still in that bun. His heart ached with love. The lights went out in the shop and it felt as if the light had gone out in his life. Hoskins locked the door and he heard them laughing as they walked, arm in arm, down the street.

He made his way back to the Green Man. Tears blinded him. Jesus, Norma, why didn't you wait? Didn't I tell you I'd be back? It'd only have been a few more shagging months. He retrieved his case and headed for the railway station.

He felt suddenly cold. He pulled the collar of his jacket up around his neck. It had started to rain again.

Epilogue

.... theirs but to reason why.

Marine Sergeant Jones snorted loudly, half-asleep, and turned over in the bed. His groping hand felt for Norma's breast. She pushed him away, wiping tears from her face with the corner of the sheet.

'No, Jack, no,' she whispered, 'you're drunk and you'll only wake Tommy.' Her husband snorted again and drifted off to sleep. She sighed. Jesus, Jesus, she thought, how did I get myself into this mess? If only you'd written more often, Jimmy! You knew I loved you. I'd have waited forever for you – me and Tommy. That's all I ever thought of - you and me and little Tommy together. But you never wrote, we thought you were dead when the war was over and you never got in touch . . .

The barmaid in the Green Man had confirmed to George that the man he described, an ex-sailor, had indeed been in the bar earlier - twice, in fact.

'Left his bag here, he did. He was ever such a nice boy. Said he was going to get married and settle down near here and open up a shop – a super-shop I think was what he called it like he'd seen in America. He was going into partnership with a mate of his who had been in the navy with him. He was so happy about it all.' She handed out two pints and wiped the counter. 'But when he came back later to collect his bag, he seemed rather upset like. Didn't have a drink or anything. Just took his bag and went. Never said where he was off to...'

Norma drowned the sobs in her throat. 'Dear God', she whispered, burying her face in the pillow, 'was it wrong to expect that a war could bring happiness to me and Tommy? Was that so wrong?' Her husband turned over and farted. Norma's head throbbed. 'Oh Jimmy, Jimmy,' she sobbed, 'why did you let this happen to us? Why? Why? Why?'

Other titles available from
Kestrel Books Ltd.

Little Old Man Cut Short
Donal O'Donovan

West Cork, 'a sort of a history, like . . .'
Tony Brehony

Irish Film - 100 Years
Arthur Flynn

Birr The Monastic City
St. Brendan of the Water Cress
Geraldine Carville

Ballads and Poems of the Wicklow Rebellion 1798
Eds: Ruan O'Donnell & Henry Cairns

Insurgent Wicklow 1798
The Story as written by Luke Cullen O.D.C.
Ed: Ruan O'Donnell

Seventeen Ninety-Eight Myth and Truth
Derry Kelleher

Wicklow Gold
Ray Cranley

St. Gerard's, Bray 1918-1998
An Educational Initiative
Brian Murphy

Buried Alive in Ireland
Derry Kelleher

Home Rule as Rome Rule
The Unspoken Unionist and Loyalist Case
Derry Kelleher

The Book of Wicklow
Arthur Flynn